Shakespeare on Management

SHAKESPEARE ON MANAGEMENT

Wise Business Counsel
from the Bard

Jay M. Shafritz

Illustrated by Seymour Chwast

HarperBusiness
A Division of HarperCollins*Publishers*

A hardcover edition of this book was published in 1992 by Birch Lane Press. It is here reprinted by arrangement with Carol Publishing Group.

HarperCollins books may be purchased for educational, business, or sales promotional use. For information please write: Special Markets Department, HarperCollins Publishers, Inc., 10 East 53rd Street, New York, NY 10022.

First HarperPerennial/HarperBusiness edition published 1999.

Designed by Arthur Hamparian

Library of Congress Cataloging-in-Publication Data

Shafritz, Jay M.
    Shakespeare on management : wise business counsel from the Bard / Jay M. Shafritz.
      p.   ill.   cm.
    Includes indexes.
    ISBN 0-06-662037-6
        1. Shakespeare, William, 1564–1616 — Knowledge — Management. 2. Shakespeare, William, 1564–1616 — Quotations. 3. Management — Quotations, maxims, etc. 4. Management in literature. I. Title
PR3069.M27S5   1999
822.3'3—dc21   99-31095

99 00 01 02 03 ❖/RRD 10 9 8 7 6 5 4 3 2 1

To Luise Alexander Shafritz
whose encouragement, criticism, editing
and love of Shakespeare (and me)
made this book possible

Contents

Introduction   xi

Dining Room Deals   1
Dressing for Success   3
Equal Opportunity   7
Estate Planning   10
Fat Versus Thin Employees   13
Flatterers and Yes Men   16
Foreign Assignments   19
Fortune Seeking   21
Getting Even   23
Glass Ceilings   26
Hierarchy   27
Informal Organizational Norms   30
Law and Lawyers   32
Life at the Top   35
Life Begins at Forty   38
Making Decisions   41
Management by Wandering Around   44
Management Information Systems   47
Management Succession   50
Marrying the Boss's Daughter   53
Meetings and Confrontations   55

Mergers and Acquisitions   58

Motivating Employees   59

Murphy's Law   63

Music and Productivity   64

Negotiating Techniques   66

New Construction   67

Office Politics   69

Organizational Behavior   73

Performance Reports   75

Personal Finance   78

Personnel Management   81

Planning   84

Policy Analysis   87

Portfolio Theory   90

Pound of Flesh   91

Practicing Business Ethics   94

Presentation Techniques   98

Promotions   101

Psychic Income   104

Public Relations   106

Retirement   108

Roles and Role Models   111

School of Hard Knocks   116

Settling Disputes   119

Spotless Reputation   121

Staff Popinjays   124

Systems Analysis   126

Timing is Everything   128

Tips and Bribes   130

Transformational Leadership   133
Unity of Command   134
Vaulting Ambition   136
Will to Succeed   139
Words of Honor and Dishonor   140
Working Stiffs   143

General Index   147
Quotation Index   152

Introduction

While William Shakespeare's contributions to literature and the development of the English language have long been acknowledged and thoroughly documented, his contributions to the theory of management and administration have been all but ignored. This is a surprising oversight when you consider that many of his plays deal with issues of personnel management and organizational behavior.

Remember *Hamlet*, the poignant case study of a too sensitive young executive who fails to move up in the organizational hierarchy because of his inability to make decisions. What is *Julius Caesar* if not a very hostile takeover attempt by disgruntled stockholders? The tragedy of *Macbeth* was that the title character was a ruthless workaholic who allowed his overly ambitious wife to egg him on to the top only to find that he couldn't hack it in the end. Who has not felt compassion when seeing *Othello*, the tale of a minority manager who incurs resentment because of his personnel policies and then finds that jealousy at the office leads to murder? And is not *King Lear* a warning to all executives of family businesses on the perils of divestiture and early retirement?

Unfortunately today's busy managers seldom have the time to read through all of Shakespeare's plays to gain the insights he offers modern business. But not to worry—I have done this work for them by creating this assembly of all his thoughts that apply to the twentieth-century business world. Managers and executives at all organizational levels can now ask themselves, "What does Shakespeare have to say about this or that business problem?" In the past there was no way to quickly find an answer. Now they need only read the appropriate chapter in *Shakespeare on Management* to learn what the great bard's advice is on dressing for success, mergers and acquisitions, motivating employees, office politics, performance reports, portfolio theory, systems analysis and much else.

Modern management has its gurus such as Peter Drucker and Tom Peters. William Shakespeare is certainly their peer. He just needs a bit of interpretation. I am reminded of a character in Molière's 1670 play, *The Would-Be Gentleman*, who suddenly said to himself one day: "Good heavens! For more than forty years I have been speaking prose without knowing it." It is the same with Shakespeare. Most managers have read or seen at least some of his plays, but have yet to realize that they have been studying management. The interpretive commentary in this book merely seeks to bring out the management that was always there in Shakespeare's works.

While sometimes meant to be humorous, this is a perfectly serious book—it is not a parody. The quotations are all real. I originally culled these excerpts from Shakespeare's plays from a wide variety of sources. I favored lightweight paperback editions of the individual plays because they were so small and fit into any pocket—ideal companions during long airplane flights and dull faculty meetings. Only after the manuscript was complete were all quotations made to conform to one particular collection, *The Riverside Shakespeare*, the most commonly used text for serious Shakespearean commentary. That is where readers can find these exact quotations. But all of the quotations, with only the most minor differences in spelling, punctuation or diction, will be found in any complete collection of Shakespeare's works.

The book is organized into short chapters on fifty-six topics of modern management, so an apt quotation can easily be found for almost any occasion or crisis. With this book always in reach, you can use Shakespeare's words to add tone, importance and especially wit to your memorandums and speeches. We can all benefit by learning more of his time-tested and truly classic executive philosophy—you never know when it might come in handy. Remember what Britain's Prince Philip is supposed to have said: "A man [or woman] can be forgiven a lot if he [or she] can quote Shakespeare in an economic crisis."

Dining Room Deals

As the Internal Revenue Service constantly regrets, many a business deal is concluded over a tax-deductible meal. It is well known that potential clients tend to be more agreeable when appropriately wined and dined. This traditional business tactic was certainly familiar to Shakespeare, who had Menenius explain in *Coriolanus* (Act V, scene i) how it is best to wait until a potential client is sated "with wine and feeding" before you "set upon him."

> He was not taken well, he had not din'd:
> The veins unfill'd, our blood is cold, and then
> We pout upon the morning, are unapt
> To give or to forgive; but when we have stuff'd
> These pipes and these conveyances of our blood
> With wine and feeding, we have suppler souls
> Than in our priest-like fasts: therefore I'll watch him
> Till he be dieted to my request,
> And then I'll set upon him.

Some clients are too wily to walk into the trap of a business meal; they may suspect that it is only an effort to manipulate them. When Bassanio invites Shylock to dine, in *The Merchant of Venice* (Act 1, scene iii), Shylock responds with this comprehensive rejection of all business sociability:

1

I will buy with you, sell with you, talk with you,
walk with you, and so following; but I will not eat
with you, drink with you, nor pray with you.

Shakespeare knew that a major problem with wining and
dining clients is the very fact that you have to eat and especially drink with them, and that the social drinking of alco-
holic beverages in business situations is not always the
pleasure people so often pretend it to be. Even though Shakespeare did not invent the "happy hour" (he used this phrase
at least half a dozen times in as many plays, though not always
in the context of drinking), he foresaw that the three-martini
lunch of today, just like the drinking bouts of yore, could have
unpleasant consequences. In *Othello* (Act II, scene iii) Cassio,
a lieutenant in the army of Venice, says:

I have very poor and unhappy brains for drinking.
I could well wish courtesy would invent some other
custom of entertainment....O God, that men
should put an enemy in their mouths to steal away
their brains! that we should, with joy, pleasance,
revel, and applause, transform ourselves into
beasts!

Shakespeare has one final piece of advice for those who
would close a deal over a meal: Be careful what you eat. In *A
Midsummer Night's Dream* (Act IV, scene ii) Bottom tells his
fellow rustic actors about to perform before royalty: "Eat no
onions nor garlic, for we are to utter sweet breath." Next time

---

2

you hear someone at a business lunch say, "Hold the onions," remember Shakespeare, that famous advocate of "sweet breath."

Dressing for Success

People in business have always sought to "dress for success." Indeed, this was the title of one of the best-selling business books of the 1970s. In *Hamlet* (Act I, scene iii) Polonius offers this advice to his grown son who is about to leave on a trip—and it is still valid for all those who seek to give a good impression:

> Costly thy habit as thy purse can buy,
> But not express'd in fancy, rich, not gaudy,
> For the apparel oft proclaims the man.

Yet Shakespeare was sophisticated enough to know that proclaiming apparel could be deceptive. As a lord says in *All's Well That Ends Well* (Act IV, scene iii):

> I will never trust a man again for keeping his sword clean, nor believe he can have every thing in him by wearing his apparel neatly.

This is reinforced by Petruchio in *The Taming of the Shrew* (Act IV, scene iii) when he says to his wife:

> Well, come, my Kate, we will unto your father's
> Even in these honest mean habiliments;
> Our purses shall be proud, our garments poor,
> For 'tis the mind that makes the body rich;
> And as the sun breaks through the darkest clouds,
> So honor peereth in the meanest habit.
> What, is the jay more precious than the lark,
> Because his feathers are more beautiful?
> Or is the adder better than the eel,
> Because his painted skin contents the eye?

The belief that clothes do not necessarily make the man was common long before Shakespeare gave it poetic expression. For example, in *Measure for Measure* (Act V, scene i) Lucio responds to a question of whether a friar was a dishonest person: "'*Cucullus non facit monachum*': honest in nothing but in his clothes." The Latin Shakespeare uses is a medieval proverb meaning: "The hood doesn't make the monk."

An astute businessperson always dresses to be inconspicuous. Few things can be as socially awkward as dressing informally when the occasion is formal and vice versa. In *The Taming of the Shrew* (Act III, scene ii) Petruchio is both late and poorly dressed for his wedding. His father-in-law-to-be, Baptista, chastises him for being an "eye-sore":

5

Why, sir, you know this is your wedding-day.
First were we sad, fearing you would not come,
Now sadder, that you come so unprovided.
Fie, doff this habit, shame to your estate [status],
An eye-sore to our solemn festival!

In Shakespeare's day as in our own, fashion sometimes demanded discomfort. An office uniform of suit and tie or high heels and pantyhose is not a pleasure for everyone to wear. Such efforts to be appropriately chic were defended by Malvolio in *Twelfth Night* (Act III, scene iv). He talks of "cross-gartering," the then fashionable practice of wearing blood-constraining garters both above and below the knee.

This does make some obstruction in the blood, this
cross-gartering, but what of that? If it please the
eye of one, it is with me as the very true sonnet is,
"Please one, and please all."

Shakespeare also knew how outrageous fashion could look. Enormous shoulder pads, flashy ruffs and ties, and too-tight tights convinced him that fashion was a "deformed thief." This is illustrated by this dialogue between Borachio and Conrade in *Much Ado About Nothing* (Act III, scene iii):

BORACHIO: Seest thou not, I say, what a deformed thief
    this fashion is, how giddily 'a turns about all the hot-
    bloods between fourteen and five-and-thirty, sometimes
    fashioning them like…the shaven Hercules in the

smirch'd worm-eaten tapestry, where his codpiece seems as massy as his club?

CONRADE: All this I see, and I see that the fashion wears out more apparel than the man.

During the Renaissance period it was common for men to wear elaborate genital coverings called codpieces. It was also common to add some strategic padding to them; hence a man's codpiece could seem "as massy [large] as his club." Then as now there were problems with truth in advertising.

Equal Opportunity

While the concept of equal employment opportunity did not exist in Shakespeare's day, he did deal with racial as well as sexual discrimination. Indeed, a common plot device had a female character dress as a man to be taken as an equal. This was all the more sexually confusing when you remember that women did not perform in Shakespeare's original productions. Adolescent boys played all the female parts. So a boy playing a woman sometimes would dress as a man who was really a woman! If you think confusion of sexual identity is not a part of modern management, just remember this case often taught in business schools. Tom, a bank teller, goes off for a few weeks of vacation and comes back as an anatomically correct Thelma. But the female tellers won't let Thelma use the women's room because they consider "him" to be a "peeping Tom." Shakespeare could have done a lot with this basic plot.

Shakespeare's most famous statements on racial and religious discrimination are in *The Merchant of Venice*. First the Prince of Morocco, "a tawny Moor," pleads (Act II, scene i):

> Mislike me not for my complexion,
> The shadowed livery of the burnish'd sun,
> To whom I am a neighbor and near bred.

Later (Act III, scene i) Shylock, a Jewish moneylender, asks:

> Hath not a Jew eyes? Hath not a Jew hands, organs,
> dimensions, senses, affections, passions; fed with
> the same food, hurt with the same weapons, subject
> to the same diseases, heal'd by the same means,
> warm'd and cool'd by the same winter and summer,
> as a Christian is?

In a parallel analysis Shakespeare makes the case for illegitimate children, a group suffering greatly, then as well as now, from legal discrimination. In *King Lear* Edmund, the illegitimate son of the Earl of Gloucester, examines (Act I, scene ii) his situation and asks the gods of equal opportunity to "stand up for bastards":

Why bastard? Wherefore base?
When my dimensions are as well compact,
My mind as generous, and my shape as true,
As honest madam's issue? Why brand they us
With base? with baseness? bastardy? base, base?
Who, in the lusty stealth of nature, take
More composition, and fierce quality,
Than doth within a dull, stale, tired bed,
Go to th' creating a whole tribe of fops,
Got 'tween asleep and wake?...
As to th' legitimate. Fine word, "legitimate"!...
Now, gods, stand up for bastards!

Today in the United States the gods of equal employment opportunity stand up for all minorities and women, for what are called "protected classes." All except bastards—for the government doesn't count them as a class worthy of special protection. However, Congressman Morris K. Udall, in his memoir, *Too Funny to Be President* (1988), tells how he sponsored a bill making illegitimate children "children" for the purposes of civil service benefits, which became informally known as the "poor bastards bill."

In spite of that irreverent appellation, or perhaps
because of it, the poor bastards bill breezed
through the House and Senate and was signed into
law....The next weekend I was in Arizona and I
met a disputatious merchant....He said,
"Congressman, you guys are throwing our money

away in Africa, Europe and everywhere else. What
I want to know is, when are you going to do
something for the poor bastards in this country?"
It was a softball question tossed from heaven. "Sir,"
I said, "I'm glad you asked that question. Why, just
last week..."

So at least some of the "gods" in the United States Congress heeded Edmund's request and did "stand up for
bastards!"

Estate Planning

The concerns of probate were very real to the Elizabethans—
especially since they tended to die sooner than we do.
Then as now the most important part of making a will was
determining your legitimate heirs. Shakespeare observed in
The Merchant of Venice (Act II, scene ii) that "it is a wise father
that knows his own child." Shakespeare was well versed in
estate planning. His own highly detailed will of 1616 is one of
the most important historical documents on his life, and his
plays show a great familiarity with wills. For example, in *The
Taming of the Shrew* Petruchio (Act II, scene i) assures his father-in-law-to-be that in consideration of his future wife's dowry, the wife will be guaranteed "her widowhood" (meaning
Petruchio's estate) upon his death:

And for that dowry, I'll assure her of
Her widowhood, be it that she survive me,
In all my lands and leases whatsoever.
Let specialties [contracts] be therefore drawn between us,
That covenants may be kept on either hand.

This is certainly a case of an early prenuptial agreement. Remember that divorce was rare in Shakespeare's day. "Till death do you part" was the norm because in any given marriage one of the partners was statistically likely to depart this world seven years after the wedding.

In *Richard II* the king (Act III, scene ii), preparing to "tell sad stories of the death of kings," says that the thing to do when contemplating death is to "choose executors and talk of wills."

Let's talk of graves, of worms, and epitaphs,
Make dust our paper, and with rainy eyes
Write sorrow on the bosom of the earth.
Let's choose executors and talk of wills;
And yet not so, for what can we bequeath
Save our deposed bodies to the ground?

The "reading of the will" scene has long been a staple of detective fiction. But it was Shakespeare who, in *Julius Caesar,* wrote the most famous will-reading scene of all time. Toward the end of the famous "Friends, Romans, countrymen" speech (Act III, scene ii) Antony incites the common people, the plebeian masses, against Caesar's assassins by telling what is in Caesar's will:

11

But here's a parchment with the seal of Caesar,
I found it in his closet, 'tis his will.
Let but the commons [the people] hear this testament—
Which, pardon me, I do not mean to read—
And they would go and kiss dead Caesar's wounds,
And dip their napkins [handkerchiefs] in his sacred
    blood;
Yea, beg a hair of him for memory,
And dying, mention it within their wills,
Bequeathing it as a rich legacy
Unto their issue....
It is not meet [proper] to know how Caesar lov'd you.
You are not wood, you are not stones, but men;
And, being men, hearing the will of Caesar,
It will inflame you, it will make you mad.
'Tis good you know not that you are his heirs;
For, if you should, O, what would come of it?...
Here is the will, and under Caesar's seal:
To every Roman citizen he gives,
To every several man, seventy-five drachmaes....
Moreover, he hath left you all his walks,
His private arbors and new-planted orchards,
On this side Tiber; he hath left them you
And to your heirs for ever—common pleasures
    [parks],
To walk abroad and recreate yourselves.
Here was a Caesar! when comes such another?

This revelation was so effective that the common people forced the assassins out of town and Antony was able to marshal support for a civil war against them. History does not record a more dramatic will reading—even in Agatha Christie! But it does record a real mystery about Shakespeare's will. In it he bequeathed his "second-best bed" to his wife. Nobody knows what happened to the *best* bed. All we know for sure was that it was Will's will.

Fat Versus Thin Employees

All upwardly mobile managers need the ability first to spot and then to cope with organizational rivals. In *Julius Caesar* (Act I, scene ii) Shakespeare offers literature's most succinct description of a now familiar figure—the highly ambitious, humorless workaholic. Caesar, who would rather have fat and contented "yes men" about him, describes the "lean and hungry" Cassius to Mark Antony:

> Let me have men about me that are fat;
> Sleek-headed men and such as sleep a-nights.
> Yond Cassius has a lean and hungry look,
> He thinks too much; such men are dangerous....
> Would he were fatter! but I fear him not.

Yet if my name were liable to fear,
I do not know the man I should avoid
So soon as that spare Cassius. He reads much,
He is a great observer, and he looks
Quite through the deeds of men. He loves no plays,
As thou dost, Antony; he hears no music;
Seldom he smiles, and smiles in such a sort
As if he mock'd himself, and scorn'd his spirit
That could be mov'd to smile at any thing.
Such men as he be never at heart's ease
Whiles they behold a greater than themselves,
And therefore are they very dangerous.

Is there a lesson here? Julius Caesar would have disagreed with what the late Duchess of Windsor is supposed to have said: "One can never be too thin or too rich." He felt that too thin was dangerous—especially to organizational rivals.

Shakespeare's Caesar would have been much more comfortable with Sir John Falstaff; but alas, they were in different plays. In *Henry IV, Part I* the Prince of Wales is assessing Sir John for a position in his future administration (when he becomes King Henry V) but (Act II, scene iv) finds him to be too fat for any job:

There is a devil haunts thee in the likeness of an
old fat man, a tun of man is thy companion. Why
dost thou converse with that trunk of humors, that
bolting-hutch of beastliness, that swoll'n parcel of

14

dropsies, that huge bombard of sack, that stuff'd cloak-bag of guts, that roasted Manningtree ox with the pudding in his belly, that reverent vice, that grey Iniquity, that father ruffian, that vanity in years? Wherein is he good, but to taste sack and drink it? wherein neat and cleanly, but to carve a capon and eat it? wherein cunning, but in craft? wherein crafty, but in villainy? wherein villanous, but in all things? wherein worthy, but in nothing?

In his own defense Sir John replies:

If sack and sugar be a fault, God help the wicked! If to be old and merry be a sin, then many an old host that I know is damn'd. If to be fat be to be hated, then Pharaoh's lean kine [cows] are to be lov'd.

Fat people are still discriminated against today. Studies constantly show that the "lean kine" are far more likely to be promoted. Equal employment opportunity laws are still not weighty enough to protect the fat: "If sack and sugar be a fault, God help the wicked," because the law won't. Sir John's hefty defense is futile. As soon as the prince rises to top management (becomes king), he cuts his old fat friend off from all contact. This is *the* classic example of deserting a long-standing friend of lesser status when one moves on to a new position of higher status. This broke Sir John's heart, and the old knight apparently died from the rejection. How-

15

ever, if someone does this to you, don't crawl off somewhere and die. Instead, immediately read this book's chapter entitled "Getting Even."

Flatterers and Yes Men

Flatterers and "yes men" have always abounded near sources of power. Insecure executives have always surrounded themselves with such aides to vanity. Confident managers know better. So does Shakespeare. In *Pericles* Helicanus (Act I, scene ii) warns:

> They do abuse [wrong] the King that flatter him,
> For flattery is the bellows blows up sin,
> The thing the which is flattered, but a spark
> To which that blast gives heat and stronger glowing;
> Whereas reproof, obedient and in order,
> Fits kings as they are men, for they may err.

Yet kings or not, there will always be those who flatter as well as those who would be flattered. In *Julius Caesar* (Act II, scene i) Decius explains how he will delay Caesar with flattery:

> he loves to hear
> That unicorns may be betray'd with trees,
> And bears with glasses [mirrors], elephants with
>   holes [pits],
> Lions with toils [nets], and men with flatterers;
> But when I tell him he hates flatterers
> He says he does, being then most flattered.

Yet flatterers are often seen through. In *Othello* (Act I, scene i) Iago describes their lives of "obsequious bondage":

> We cannot all be masters, nor all masters
> Cannot be truly follow'd. You shall mark
> Many a duteous and knee-crooking knave
> That (doting on his own obsequious bondage)
> Wears out his time, much like his master's ass,
> For nought but provender [fodder], and when
>   he's old, cashier'd.
> Whip me such honest knaves.

But Shakespeare's most extended analysis of flatterers comes not from any of his plays, but from the last part of his poem *The Passionate Pilgrim*.

> Every one that flatters thee
> Is no friend in misery.
> Words are easy, like the wind,
> Faithful friends are hard to find:
> Every man will be thy friend,

Whilst thou hast wherewith to spend;
But if store of crowns be scant,
No man will supply thy want....
He that is thy friend indeed,
He will help thee in thy need:
If thou sorrow, he will weep;
If thou wake, he cannot sleep;
Thus of every grief in heart
He with thee doth bear a part.
These are certain signs to know
Faithful friend from flatt'ring foe.

Finally, there is that familiar remark on the appropriate amount of flattery to use. Celia, in *As You Like It* (Act I, scene ii), responds to a bit of flattery by saying, "Well said—that was laid on with a trowel." This was famously enhanced by nineteenth-century British prime minister Benjamin Disraeli: "Everyone likes flattery; and when you come to royalty you should lay it on with a trowel." Organizational royalty, the highest executives, are just as susceptible to having it laid on. But when the time comes that you are on the receiving end, always remember that your position is being flattered—not you.

Foreign Assignments

As business becomes more and more internationalized, foreign assignments become increasingly commonplace for senior managers. Shakespeare knew that there were few greater stresses than suddenly to be forced to live in an alien nation. Then as now the foremost problem was coping with foreign languages—something that Americans especially have been most reluctant to do. In *Richard II* (Act I, scene iii) Thomas Mowbray is ordered exiled, forcibly transferred to a foreign land. In a last appeal to the king he complains of being sent to "speechless death":

> The language I have learnt these forty years,
> My native English, now I must forgo,
> And now my tongue's use is to me no more
> Than an unstringed viol or a harp,
> Or like a cunning instrument cas'd up,
> Or being open, put into his hands
> That knows no touch to tune the harmony.
> Within my mouth you have enjail'd my tongue,
> Doubly portcullis'd with my teeth and lips,
> And dull unfeeling barren ignorance
> Is made my jailer to attend on me.
> I am too old to fawn upon a nurse,
> Too far in years to be a pupil now.
> What is thy sentence then but speechless death,
> Which robs my tongue from breathing native breath?

Shakespeare's characters often had trouble with foreign languages, particularly French. In *Henry V* (Act V, scene ii) King Henry, while on a foreign assignment to conquer France, handily defeats the flower of French nobility at the Battle of Agincourt. But he has a seemingly far more difficult task in convincing Katherine, the daughter of the defeated French king, to marry him. As he woos her in decidedly faulty French, he complains:

> I will tell thee in French, which I am sure will hang
> upon my tongue like a new-married wife about her
> husband's neck, hardly to be shook off....It is as
> easy for me, Kate, to conquer the kingdom as to
> speak so much more French. I shall never move
> thee in French, unless it be to laugh at me.

She does laugh at his French but marries him anyway. She didn't really have a choice. It's almost the same if you are a modern executive in a foreign post. But *you do* have a choice—you can learn the foreign language or you can risk having your business laughed away.

Fortune Seeking

Business is commonly defined as an activity in which individuals, at the risk of loss, seek profit. Shakespeare understood how important it was to take advantage of a business opportunity, to embrace fortune when it presented itself. In *Julius Caesar* (Act IV, scene iii) Brutus ponders taking the "tide" that might lead "on to fortune":

> There is a tide in the affairs of men,
> Which taken at the flood, leads on to fortune;
> Omitted, all the voyage of their life
> Is bound in shallows and in miseries.
> On such a full sea are we now afloat,
> And we must take the current when it serves,
> Or lose our ventures.

Poor Brutus took the wrong tide and ended up a suicide. But at least he tried. When you consider that more than half of all new businesses started in the United States will fail within five years, you realize that entrepreneurs face horrendous odds. Yet they are highly motivated by the prospect of great rewards. As the Prince of Morocco states in *The Merchant of Venice* (Act II, scene vii):

> Men that hazard all
> Do it in hope of fair advantages;
> A golden mind stoops not to shows of dross [rubbish].

Naturally we all try to steer toward good fortune. Sometimes we get there, sometimes not. Often success is just dumb luck, as Pisanio in *Cymbeline* observes (Act IV, scene iii): "Fortune brings in some boats that are not steer'd." It is easy to bear good fortune. But what about ill fortune? Would someone have to say of you what Iago says in *Othello* (Act IV, scene i): "Would you would bear your fortune like a man!" We are taught to behave calmly and stoically ("like a man") in the face of ill tidings. Ironically, that is when we most want to run away and cry, like the inconsolate, bawling Romeo in *Romeo and Juliet* (Act III, scene iii). Friar Lawrence chastizes him:

> Hold thy desperate hand!
> Art thou a man? Thy form cries out thou art;
> Thy tears are womanish, thy wild acts denote
> The unreasonable fury of a beast.
> Unseemly woman in a seeming man,
> And ill-beseeming beast in seeming both.

There is a lesson here. People will think less of you if you can't handle bad news without unseemly emotion. So even when there may be good reason to do so, don't cry at the office.

Chances must be taken to achieve goals. Consequently it is all the more important that these gains are worth achieving. The acquisition of a new company or product line that seems tactically wise at the time can turn out to be strategically imprudent if it does not eventually generate appropriate profits. Wise investors will always seek to avoid the kind of acquisitions or properties described by a Norwegian captain to Prince Hamlet in *Hamlet* (Act IV, scene iv):

> Truly to speak, and with no addition [detail],
> We go to gain a little patch of ground
> That hath in it no profit but the name.

Of course, sometimes there can be great profit in a name alone. Designers, such as Bill Blass or Oscar de la Renta, sometimes license their names to be used on products they did not directly design. Or a manufacturer of one product may use its name for related merchandise: thus Levi's, famous at first only for jeans, now makes shoes, shirts, and socks as well. Shakespeare would have immediately understood this concept of brand extension; he just would have put it in terms of territorial conquests. Same thing, really!

Getting Even

"**D**on't get mad, get even" is a much honored maxim of organizational life. This philosophic disposition, that one bad turn deserves another, was never better expressed than in *The Merchant of Venice* (Act III, scene i). Shylock asks:

If you prick us, do we not bleed? If you tickle us, do we not laugh? If you poison us, do we not die? And if you wrong us, shall we not revenge?

He then proclaims:

The villainy you teach me, I will execute, and it shall go hard but I will better the instruction.

A decade after Shakespeare wrote *The Merchant of Venice*, he wrote *Macbeth,* wherein he picks up on this theme of teaching "bloody instructions." Macbeth (Act I, scene vii) worries that his evil doings might backfire on him. As he contemplates murdering King Duncan he muses:

> that but this blow
> Might be the be-all and the end-all—here,
> But here, upon this bank and shoal of time,
> We'd jump [risk] the life to come. But in these cases
> We still have judgment here, that we but teach
> Bloody instructions, which, being taught, return
> To plague th' inventor. This even-handed justice
> Commends th' ingredience of our poison'd chalice
> To our own lips.

Macbeth's fears proved true. The chain of events he started with his "bloody instructions" led, by the end of the fifth act, to his own death. The revenge tragedy, in which one murder leads in succession to the killing of most of the cast by the end of the play, was a popular genre in Elizabethan drama. Both *Macbeth* and *Hamlet* fall into this category. Remember that the plot of *Hamlet* really begins (Act I, scene v) when Hamlet meets his father's ghost on the battlements of Elsinore castle:

GHOST: Pity me not, but lend thy serious hearing
              To what I shall unfold.
HAMLET: Speak, I am bound to hear.
GHOST: So art thou to revenge, when thou shalt hear.

The ghost then explains how his brother, Claudius, took over the family business, the kingdom, by murdering *his* brother, Hamlet's father. Hamlet is thus charged by the ghost, his father, with taking back the firm. His indecisiveness about this takes up most of the play. By the final curtain, all the principal characters are dead. That's the problem with getting even—all too often people you don't want to hurt, like your mother, do get hurt. So what's the answer? The answer is: Don't be indecisive. Kill your uncle in the first act; then you and your mother will still be alive by the end of the fifth. This is advice as old as Machiavelli. When you take over an organization, get rid of your natural rivals. Such an initial bloodletting can save a lot of blood later on—and the blood you save may be your own.

Glass Ceilings

The glass ceiling is a current term for the sex discrimination that seems to keep women as a group from rising to the top ranks in corporations and organizations. They can see to the top (thus the glass), but they can't get through to it (thus the ceiling). Lady Macbeth in *Macbeth* (Act I, scene v) complains that her female sex inhibits her from advancing in life, from becoming as nasty as she longs to be. So she asks the "spirits" to "unsex me here," to do away with her feminine side and make her more like the murderous man she would make of herself:

> Come, you spirits
> That tend on mortal thoughts, unsex me here,
> And fill me from the crown to the toe topful
> Of direst cruelty! Make thick my blood,
> Stop up th' access and passage to remorse,
> That no compunctious visitings of nature
> Shake my fell purpose, nor keep peace between
> Th' effect and it! Come to my woman's breasts,
> And take my milk for gall.

Nevertheless, sometimes a totally unscrupulous manlike "lady" like Lady Macbeth is just what is needed to get the job done—especially in tough times. Still, there will always be those who argue that women shouldn't go about murdering kings or otherwise straying from domestic pursuits. This is

---

26

the attitude Katherine, the shrew, takes toward the end of *The Taming of the Shrew* when she is happily married to Petruchio. She tells the women of Padua (Act V, scene ii):

> I am asham'd that women are so simple
> To offer war where they should kneel for peace,
> Or seek for rule, supremacy, and sway,
> When they are bound to serve, love, and obey.
> Why are our bodies soft, and weak, and smooth,
> Unapt to toil and trouble in the world,
> But that our soft conditions, and our hearts,
> Should well agree with our external parts?

This was one shrew who was certainly tamed. By the play's end she wouldn't know a glass ceiling if she fell through one.

Hierarchy

Shakespeare was well acquainted with the bureaucratic structuring of modern organizations. What else could Hamlet have meant when in *Hamlet* (Act III, scene i) he refers to "the insolence of office"? Obviously this is one of the earliest instances of "bureaucrat bashing."

In two other plays, Shakespeare provides portraits of bureaucratized societies using the metaphor of a beehive. In *Troilus and Cressida* Ulysses (Act I, scene iii) uses the image of the hive to describe the hierarchical structure of Greek military society:

When that the general [society] is not like the hive
To whom the foragers shall all repair,
What honey is expected? Degree being vizarded [hidden],
Th' unworthiest shows as fairly in the mask.
The heavens themselves, the planets, and this centre [earth]
Observe degree, priority, and place,
Insisture [regularity], course, proportion, season, form,
Office, and custom, in all line of order.

Shakespeare, an organizational conservative, was greatly concerned that established hierarchies be maintained. Thus he has Ulysses explain later in this same speech what happens when the elements of a system fall out of their "line of order":

But when the planets
In evil mixture to disorder wander,
What plagues and what portents, what mutiny!

In *Henry V* the Archbishop of Canterbury explains (Act I, scene ii) how heaven has ordained a hierarchically ordered universe wherein each person is assigned an occupational specialization, a social rank and formal obligations:

Therefore doth heaven divide
The state of man in divers functions,
Setting endeavor in continual motion;
To which is fixed, as an aim or butt,
Obedience; for so work the honey-bees,
Creatures that by a rule in nature teach
The act of order to a peopled kingdom.
They have a king, and officers of sorts,
Where some, like magistrates, correct at home;
Others, like merchants, venture trade abroad;
Others, like soldiers, armed in their stings,
Make boot upon the summer's velvet buds,
Which pillage they with merry march bring home
To the tent-royal of their emperor.

Note how Shakespeare anticipates the concept of division of labor: "heaven divide[s]...man in divers functions." Later in this same long speech, the archbishop further develops this idea:

As many fresh streams meet in one salt sea;
As many lines close in the dial's [sundial's] centre;
So may a thousand actions, once afoot,
End in one purpose.

Yet books on the history of organization theory generally credit Adam Smith with pioneering this concept in his *Wealth of Nations* (1776). It just goes to show you that Smith, the "father of economics," was a disciple of Shakespeare, the father of organization theory.

Informal Organizational Norms

Virtually every student in every introductory course on management learns of the Hawthorne experiments made by the Harvard Business School at the Hawthorne Works of the Western Electric Company during the late 1920s and early 1930s. The researchers stumbled upon a finding that today seems so obvious—factories and other work situations are, first of all, social situations. Thus managers, if they are to be optimally effective, have to be aware of the informal as well as the formal organization. Of course, Shakespeare had already shown that those managers who must rely only upon formal authority are at a disadvantage when compared to those competitors who can also mobilize the informal strength of their organizations. In *Macbeth* (Act V, scene ii) Angus describes Macbeth's waning ability to command the loyalty of his troops:

> Those he commands move only in command,
> Nothing in love. Now does he feel his title
> Hang loose about him, like a giant's robe
> Upon a dwarfish thief.

Any manager whose title hangs "loose about him" (or her) does not command the full potential of his or her organization; he or she cannot inspire motivation, only order movement. The same loss of an organization's full potential occurs if managers allow discipline to become too lax. In *Measure for Measure,* the duke (Act I, scene iii) offers this

---

30

lamenting description of a society where the informal norms developed over time have made "biting laws" things to be "more mock'd than fear'd":

> We have strict statutes and most biting laws...
> Which for this fourteen years we have let slip,
> Even like an o'ergrown lion in a cave,
> That goes not out to prey. Now, as fond fathers,
> Having bound up the threat'ning twigs of birch,
> Only to stick it in their children's sight
> For terror, not to use, in time the rod
> Becomes more mock'd than fear'd; so our decrees,
> Dead to infliction, to themselves are dead,
> And liberty [license] plucks justice by the nose;
> The baby beats the nurse, and quite athwart
> Goes all decorum.

Shakespeare's most famous acknowledgment of the importance of informal norms occurs in *Hamlet* (Act I, scene iv) when the Danish royal court drinks toasts to the accompaniment of drums and trumpets. Horatio, startled by this unusually noisy practice, asks Hamlet if this is "a custom." Hamlet replies:

> But to my mind, though I am native here
> And to the manner born, it is a custom
> More honor'd in the breach than the observance.

Thus Shakespeare has explained that although formal

procedures are in place, the organization sensibly ignores them. Often this is for the good. Western literature is full of examples of servants not obeying stupid or ill-advised orders from their masters. As Posthumus asserts in *Cymbeline* (Act V, scene i):

> Every good servant does not all commands;
> No bond, but to do just ones.

Perhaps you should quote this to your boss the next time you are ordered to do something particularly ill-advised. But since not all bosses take well to criticism, maybe you should just leave this book open to this page on his or her desk instead!

Law and Lawyers

Many people are familiar with what they think is Shake-speare's recommendation on what to do with the entire legal profession: "Let's kill all the lawyers" (*Henry VI, Part II*, Act IV, scene ii). But probably only a comparative few know the context of this statement. It is spoken by Dick the Butcher, one of the followers of Jack Cade, the utopian rabble-rouser who aspires to the throne of England. Here is the revolutionary rhetoric of Cade and Dick:

CADE: ...there shall be no money; all shall eat and drink on my score, and I will apparel them all in one livery, that they may agree like brothers, and worship me their lord.

DICK: The first thing we do, let's kill all the lawyers.

CADE: Nay, that I mean to do. Is not this a lamentable thing, that of the skin of an innocent lamb should be made parchment? that parchment, being scribbled o'er, should undo a man?

This murderous remark was made by one of the dregs of Elizabethan society at what amounts to a meeting of anarchists, totalitarian communists or worse; Shakespeare surely did not mean that it should be taken seriously. Of course, one can only be sympathetic to Shakespeare's vision of "innocent lamb[s]" dying throughout the land so that legal papers can "undo a man."

But Shakespeare didn't just make cheap jokes at the expense of lawyers; his plays demonstrate a very sophisticated knowledge of law in general and business law in particular. They show such a deep understanding of law that some scholars have speculated that he must have had legal training. Shakespeare certainly knew the law was often corrupt. For example, in *Hamlet* King Claudius muses (Act III, scene iii):

> In the corrupted currents of this world
> Offense's gilded hand may shove by justice,
> And oft 'tis seen the wicked prize itself
> Buys out the law.

Claudius knew from experience that with the things he stole—"the wicked prize"—he could "buy out the law." Even if the law is not bought directly through the time-honored (although not honorable) technique of bribery, it can still be bought indirectly by the "seasoned and gracious voice" of a high-priced lawyer. As Bassanio explains in *The Merchant of Venice* (Act III, scene ii):

> The world is still deceiv'd with ornament.
> In law, what plea so tainted and corrupt
> But, being season'd with a gracious voice,
> Obscures the show of evil?

Yet the same Shakespeare who showed cynicism about the law could also show idealism. In *Measure for Measure* (Act II, scene i) Angelo asserts:

> We must not make a scarecrow of the law,
> Setting it up to fear [frighten] the birds of prey,
> And let it keep one shape, till custom make it
> Their perch and not their terror.

A constant theme in Shakespeare's plays is the restoration of legitimate legal authority. Many of his villains (such as Richard III or Coriolanus) and tragic figures (such as Macbeth and Lady Macbeth) sought to upset the natural order. Shakespeare was a conservative. In his world, usurpers never won—unless, of course, like Henry IV, they were relatives of Elizabeth I. The Elizabethan theater was bawdy and boisterous, but it was not a bastion of free speech. Criticism of the queen or her antecedent relations was considered treason. One is reminded of an epigram written by one of Shakespeare's contemporaries, John Harington:

> Treason doth never prosper:
>   What's the reason?
> For if it prosper, none dare
>   Call it treason.

Life at the Top

Top executives often tend to make it as hard as possible for others to follow their paths to success—perhaps because they fear possible rivals. Shakespeare knew that those who succeed in rising to the heights of their organization's pyramid often spend an inordinate amount of time worrying about being supplanted by those with more youthful ambitions. In *Julius Caesar* (Act II, scene i) Brutus observes this all too common phenomenon:

But 'tis a common proof
That lowliness is young ambition's ladder,
Whereto the climber-upward turns his face;
But when he once attains the upmost round [rung],
He then unto the ladder turns his back,
Looks in the clouds, scorning the base degrees
By which he did ascend.

Almost inexplicably, executives spend most of their working lives striving to get to the top but, once they are there, tend to complain about the demands of high office. This burden is best summarized by Laertes in *Hamlet* (Act I, scene iii), when he explains to his little sister, Ophelia, the executive burdens that fall upon Prince Hamlet:

His greatness weigh'd, his will is not his own,
For he himself is subject to his birth:
He may not, as unvalued persons do,
Carve [decide] for himself, for on his choice depends
The safety and health of this whole state,
And therefore must his choice be circumscrib'd
Unto the voice and yielding of that body [the state]
Whereof he is the head.

Shakespeare once again uses the theme that an executive's life is not his own in *Henry V* (Act IV, scene i). In a long soliloquy King Henry contemplates his position as king and compares himself unfavorably to a "wretched slave." With a change in diction this could be the complaint of any chief

executive officer whose day is constantly overscheduled with
ceremonial events:

> What infinite heart's ease
> Must kings neglect, that private men enjoy!
> And what have kings, that privates have not too,
> Save ceremony, save general ceremony?
> And what art thou, thou idol Ceremony?...
> O Ceremony, show me but thy worth!
> What is thy soul [secret] of adoration?
> Art thou aught else but place, degree, and form,
> Creating awe and fear in other men?
> Wherein thou art less happy, being fear'd,
> Than they in fearing.
> What drink'st thou oft, in stead of homage sweet,
> But poison'd flattery?...
> 'Tis not the balm, the sceptre, and the ball,
> The sword, the mace, the crown imperial,
> The intertissued robe of gold and pearl,
> The farced [pompous] title running 'fore the King,
> The throne he sits on, nor the tide of pomp
> That beats upon the high shore of this world—
> No, not all these, thrice-gorgeous ceremony,
> Not all these, laid in bed majestical,
> Can sleep so soundly as the wretched slave;
> Who, with a body fill'd and vacant mind,
> Gets him to rest, cramm'd with distressful
>   [hard-earned] bread,...
> And, but for ceremony, such a wretch,

Winding up days with toil and nights with sleep,
Had the forehand [superior position] and vantage
[advantage] of a king.

The totality of this executive angst is famously summarized by King Henry IV in *Henry IV, Part II* (Act III, scene i) when he complains, "Uneasy lies the head that wears the crown." But if being top dog is such a hard life, why do so many yelp for it? Because of, as American psychologist William James wrote, "the moral flabbiness born of the exclusive worship of the bitch-goddess SUCCESS. That—with the squalid cash interpretation put on the word success—is our national disease."

Life Begins at Forty

S ophie Tucker (1884–1966), the singer who billed herself as "the last of the red-hot mamas," was famous in her later years for telling her increasingly older audiences that "life begins at forty." Yet many employers, fearful of low productivity or pension obligations, developed discriminatory policies toward such seasoned workers. This led the federal government (as well as many state governments) to pass laws prohibiting discrimination against employees over age forty. Shakespeare knew that forty was an age when people were considered old and consequently "of small worth held." He wrote in the second of his sonnets (1609):

> When forty winters shall besiege thy brow,
> And dig deep trenches in thy beauty's field,
> Thy youth's proud livery, so gaz'd on now,
> Will be a totter'd weed [tattered garment] of
> small worth held.

Note, however, that Shakespeare only mentions superficial perceptions. He does not say that those over forty are of small worth, only that they are considered of small worth. Of course, age is always relative. A young King Henry V in *Henry V* (Act V, scene ii) asserts: "The elder I wax, the better I shall appear."

Other characters felt obliged to deny that their old age impaired their abilities. For example, Adam, a servant in *As You Like It* (Act II, scene iii), applies for a new position with this plea:

> let me be your servant.
> Though I look old, yet I am strong and lusty;
> For in my youth I never did apply
> Hot and rebellious liquors in my blood,
> Nor did not with unbashful forehead woo
> The means of weakness and debility;
> Therefore my age is as a lusty winter,
> Frosty, but kindly. Let me go with you,
> I'll do the service of a younger man
> In all your business and necessities.

Some biographers suggest that Shakespeare himself, a sometime actor, played this role in the original production in 1600. By then he would have been approaching forty.

Occasionally employees cope with age discrimination by lying about their age. In *Henry IV, Part II* (Act I, scene ii) Sir John Falstaff tries to excuse his misdemeanors before a judge by claiming that because he, Falstaff, is so young, the judge is too old to understand him. The judge doesn't buy this logic and observes how Sir John is "blasted with antiquity."

SIR JOHN FALSTAFF: You that are old consider not the capacities of us that are young, you do measure the heat of our livers with the bitterness of your galls....

CHIEF JUSTICE: Do you set down your name in the scroll of youth, that are written down old with all the characters of age? Have you not a moist eye, a dry hand, a yellow cheek, a white beard, a decreasing leg, an increasing belly? Is not your voice broken, your wind short, your chin double, your wit single, and every part about you blasted with antiquity? and will you yet call yourself young? Fie, fie, fie, Sir John!

SIR JOHN FALSTAFF: My lord, I was born about three of the clock in the afternoon, with a white head and something [of] a round belly. For my voice, I have lost it with hallowing and singing of anthems. To approve my youth further, I will not. The truth is, I am only old in judgment and understanding.

Shakespeare understood that "life begins at forty" because his years after forty were among his most productive, as they can be with modern executives who are really "only old in judgment and understanding." In today's organizations you don't have to write a *King Lear* or *Macbeth,* as Shakespeare did when he was over forty; you need only demonstrate that you can still put on a show at the office.

Making Decisions

It is a truism in management that it is better to make a wrong decision once in a while than to be constantly indecisive. Many of Shakespeare's characters grapple with indecisiveness to their detriment. It is Prince Hamlet who in *Hamlet* (Act III, scene i) makes what has become literature's definitive statement on indecisiveness:

> To be, or not to be, that is the question:
> Whether 'tis nobler in the mind to suffer
> The slings and arrows of outrageous fortune,
> Or to take arms against a sea of troubles,
> And by opposing, end them.

Although poor Hamlet is the most famous indecisive character in Shakespeare, he had considerable company. For example, Isabella in *Measure for Measure* (Act II, scene ii) complains that "I am at war 'twixt will and will not." And the Earl of Northumberland in *Henry IV, Part II* (Act II, scene iii) cries out:

> 'Tis with my mind
> As with the tide swell'd up unto his height,
> That makes a still-stand, running neither way.

Sometimes Shakespearean characters, much as in real life, have a spouse who will help them make up their minds. Was ever a wife more helpful than Lady Macbeth? When her husband seems indecisive about undertaking the murder of King Duncan, in *Macbeth* (Act I, scene vii), she kindly reassures him:

MACBETH: If we should fail?
LADY MACBETH: We fail?
                But screw your courage to the sticking
                    place,
                And we'll not fail.

Some readers have found a blatant lewdness in her instructions. And there has been much speculation about just where Lady Macbeth thought the proper "sticking place" was. Nevertheless, her advice worked; Macbeth eventually became a very successful murderer, at least until the last act.

The key to success, whether for a character in Shakespeare or a player in modern business, lies in overcoming indecisiveness. As Lucio asserts in *Measure for Measure* (Act I, scene iv):

> Our doubts are traitors,
> And make us lose the good we oft might win,
> By fearing to attempt.

Such a paralyzing fear of action confines many employees to jobs below those to which they aspire. Complaints are heard of bad luck or poor training. But Shakespeare knew, as he has Cassius tell "dear Brutus" in *Julius Caesar* (Act I, scene ii):

> Men at some time are masters of their fates;
> The fault, dear Brutus, is not in our stars,
> But in ourselves, that we are underlings.

Yet people still yearn to blame the fates or their stars for their personal inadequacies or misfortunes. In *King Lear* (Act I, scene ii) Edmund states that we all have a tendency toward celestial scapegoating:

> This is the excellent foppery [foolishness] of the
> world, that when we are sick in fortune—often the
> surfeit of our own behavior—we make guilty of our
> disasters the sun, the moon, and stars: as if we were
> villains on necessity, fools by heavenly compulsion,

knaves, thieves, and treachers [traitors] by spherical [celestial] predominance; drunkards, liars, and adulterers by an enforc'd obedience of planetary influence; and all that we are evil in by a divine thrusting on. An admirable evasion of whoremaster man, to lay his goatish disposition on the charge of a star!

So next time you have a problem at work, don't blame "the sun, the moon, and stars." Shakespeare was wise to that tactic, and so, probably, is your boss.

Management by Wandering Around

Tom Peters, the best-selling author of *In Search of Excellence* (1982) and *Thriving on Chaos* (1987), is a strong advocate of "management by wandering around." This calls for an executive to test the accuracy of reporting systems by making random visits to employee work sites to gain information about what is really happening—as opposed to what the various levels of middle management say is happening. As Peters puts it: "You must visit and chat with these knowledgeable people where and when the action is—at 3 a.m. on the loading dock," for example. This is exactly what Shakespeare has King Henry do on the eve of the Battle of Agincourt in 1415. In *Henry V* (Act IV, scene i) the king, knowing that his army must fight the French in the morning, borrows a cloak to disguise himself so that he may randomly roam about the campfires of his troops and take their measure. The Chorus (the narrator) calls this "a little touch of Harry in the night."

The information he gains by wandering around, mainly that the men are fearful because they are massively outnumbered, he uses in his famous "St. Crispin's Day" speech (Act IV, scene iii) to his troops on the morning of battle. He begins by addressing the fact that they are but one to three:

> If we are mark'd to die, we are enow [enough]
> To do our country loss; and if to live,
> The fewer men, the greater share of honor.

Then he turns their numerical inferiority to advantage with one of the best-known motivational speeches in all of English literature—made all the more memorable because it celebrates one of England's greatest victories.

> This day is call'd the feast of Crispian:
> He that outlives this day, and comes safe home,
> Will stand a' tiptoe when this day is named,
> And rouse him at the name of Crispian.
> He that shall see this day, and live old age,
> Will yearly on the vigil feast his neighbors,
> And say, "To-morrow is Saint Crispian."

Then will he strip his sleeve and show his scars,
And say, "These wounds I had on Crispin's day."
Old men forget; yet all shall be forgot,
But he'll remember with advantages
What feats he did that day. Then shall our names,
Familiar in his mouth as household words,
Harry the King, Bedford and Exeter,
Warwick and Talbot, Salisbury and Gloucester,
Be in their flowing [brimming] cups freshly rememb'red.
This story shall the good man teach his son;
And Crispin Crispian shall ne'er go by,
From this day to the ending of the world,
But we in it shall be remembered—
We few, we happy few, we band of brothers;
For he to-day that sheds his blood with me
Shall be my brother; be he ne'er so vile [lower-class],
This day shall gentle his condition;
And gentlemen in England, now a-bed,
Shall think themselves accurs'd they were not here;
And hold their manhoods cheap whiles any speaks
That fought with us upon Saint Crispin's day.

It is interesting to compare Henry's offer of perpetual glory to General George S. Patton's parallel statement to American troops just before D-Day in 1944:

There's one great thing you men can say when it's all over and you're home once more. You can thank God that twenty years from now, when you're

sitting around the fireside with your grandson on
your knee and he asks you what you did in the war,
you won't have to shift him to the other knee,
cough, and say, "I shoveled shit in Louisiana."

Shakespeare, the managerial psychologist par excellence, knew that leaders had to offer the positive reinforcement of glory (or wealth) as opposed to the negative reinforcement of merely not having been a Louisiana shoveler; that the manager who wanders around has to discover what reinforcements are needed—and provide them.

Management Information Systems

Nothing is more critical to modern business than timely and accurate management information systems. Top executives must be kept informed of possible problems within their organizations. How else can they know what action to take? But today, as in Shakespeare's time, subordinates are reluctant to bring bad news to the top. They know, as the Earl of Northumberland observes in *Henry IV, Part II* (Act I, scene i):

Yet the first bringer of unwelcome news
Hath but a losing office, and his tongue
Sounds ever after as a sullen bell,
Rememb'red tolling a departing friend.

Subordinates have long known that it is "but a losing office" to be the bearer of bad tidings. Cleopatra in *Antony and Cleopatra* was particularly annoyed when bad news wasn't brought to her in the most diplomatic manner. The Queen of the Nile flew into a rage (Act II, scene v) when a messenger said, "But yet, madam...":

I do not like "but yet," it does allay [qualify]
The good precedence; fie upon "but yet"!
"But yet" is as a jailer to bring forth
Some monstrous malefactor. Prithee, friend,
Pour out the pack of matter to mine ear,
The good and bad together.

Later in that same scene she commits one of the greatest of all management mistakes. She tells her staff not to inform her of bad news until it is too late to remedy the situation:

Though it be honest, it is never good
To bring bad news. Give to a gracious message
An host of tongues, but let ill tidings tell
Themselves when they be felt.

Cleopatra's lover, Antony, knew that this head-in-the-sand attitude was no way to run an empire. Consider Antony's contrasting dialogue (Act I, scene ii) with one of his messengers:

ANTONY: Well, what worst?
MESSENGER: The nature of bad news infects the teller.
ANTONY: When it concerns the fool or coward. On:
                        Things that are past are done with me.
                           'Tis thus:
                        Who tells me true, though in his tale lie
                           death,
                        I hear him as he flatter'd....
                        Speak to me home [plainly], mince not the
                           general tongue.

Antony the soldier knew the importance of truthful intelligence. He would not let bad news harm the teller of it. A good manager needs to know the bad even sooner than the good. Cleopatra, in contrast, refused to hear the bad until it was even worse—a surprising failure of savvy in a ruler who was reported to be quite intelligent.

Management Succession

The problem of management succession was an Elizabethan obsession, all the more troubling because Elizabeth I was the Virgin Queen. Thus many of Shakespeare's plays dealt with the hot topic of succession. Often Shakespeare illustrated the corporate raider approach—in plays such as *Macbeth, Richard II* and *Richard III,* ambitious subordinates climb up the corporate ladder as they knock off all rivals. But Shakespeare also offered moving examinations of the kind of peaceful management succession still common today: the ordinary transfer of power as children take over the family business or family kingdom.

King Lear is both an example of just such a peaceful transfer and an object lesson on how not to do it. King Lear (Act I, scene i) announces his retirement and tells his children:

> I do invest you jointly with my power,
> Pre-eminence, and all the large effects
> That troop with majesty. Ourself, by monthly course,
> With reservation of an hundred knights
> By you to be sustain'd, shall our abode
> Make with you by due turn. Only we shall retain
> The name, and all th' addition [honors due] to a king.

Here, in essence, is the patriarch of a huge family enterprise turning over the business to his children—except that he'll keep the title of chief executive officer and a personal staff of a hundred. That this was no way to run a railroad or a kingdom was evident even then. As Lear's daughter Goneril later tells him (Act I, scene iv): "As you are old and reverend, you should be wise." But one lesson at the heart of the play is that age, unfortunately, does not necessarily bring wisdom.

It is always pitiful when death forces a patriarch to yield a family business to a child who is considered unworthy or unable. This was the case in *Henry IV, Part II.* The dying King Henry IV (Act IV, scene v) says to his son, the future Henry V:

> I stay too long by thee, I weary thee.
> Dost thou so hunger for mine empty chair
> That thou wilt needs invest thee with my honors
> Before thy hour be ripe? O foolish youth,
> Thou seek'st the greatness that will overwhelm thee.

Then he offers his son this final piece of management advice:

> Come hither, Harry, sit thou by my bed,
> And hear (I think) the very latest counsel
> That ever I shall breathe. God knows, my son,
> By what by-paths and indirect crook'd ways
> I met this crown, and I myself know well
> How troublesome it sate [sat] upon my head.
> To thee it shall descend with better quiet,
> Better opinion, better confirmation,
> For all the soil of the achievement goes
> With me into the earth.

King Henry has told his son how much easier it will be for him to manage because "all the soil of the achievement"—the dirty work in building the family business—has been done by the father's generation. Thus the son will have "better opinion," a better reputation with the business community and the public. This is a common drama in real-life business and politics. The first-generation robber barons (such as the Rockefellers or the Harrimans) bequeathed to their children an industrial empire and took their soiled reputations for "crook'd ways" to their graves, "into the earth." This freed the younger generation to give lectures on the social responsibility of business or run for president. As for the despicable ways in which daddy originally gained the family fortune— well, those crimes, those issues, are all dead and buried with the old man. A remarkable convenience! This situation calls for the question asked by King Henry in *Henry VI, Part III* (Act II, scene ii):

> And happy always was it for the son
> Whose father for his hoarding went to hell?

Marrying the Boss's Daughter

A truly classic technique for getting ahead in business is to marry the boss's daughter. Those who have criticized this method were probably never presented with such an opportunity. In Shakespeare's *The Taming of the Shrew* (Act I, scene ii) Petruchio, a young man who has just arrived in Padua to find a wife, openly brags:

> I come to wive it wealthily in Padua;
> If wealthily, then happily in Padua.

If these lines sound familiar, it may be because they were set to music by Cole Porter in his 1948 musical *Kiss Me Kate*.

Often matrimonial efforts at career advancement have happy endings. Petruchio did "wive it wealthily in Padua" with Katherine. And after the stormiest period of adjustment in the literature of the Western world, they wound up happy together. Some fortune seekers, however, are lucky enough to have a happy marriage from the start. For example, consider Fenton in *The Merry Wives of Windsor* (Act III, scene iv) as he tells Anne Page of his initial motives in wooing her:

> Albeit I will confess thy father's wealth
> Was the first motive that I woo'd thee, Anne;
> Yet wooing thee, I found thee of more value
> Than stamps in gold, or sums in sealed bags;
> And 'tis the very riches of thyself
> That now I aim at.

This line works for Fenton. Anne learns to love him in spite of his initial motives, and they marry later in the play. Of course, this confessional approach may not work today unless the girl's name is Gullible. Nevertheless, marrying into the boss's family still works. Ask Charles S. Robb. This young Marine Corps officer married the daughter of his boss, the president of the United States (Lyndon B. Johnson), in a much publicized White House wedding. Her family connections and money helped him to become Virginia's lieutenant governor, governor and then U.S. senator. A talented man, to be sure; but had he not married Lynda Bird Johnson, we might never have heard of him. It's no different in the corporate world: Talent is essential, but access makes the difference. When Petruchio first wooed Katherine in *The Taming of the Shrew,* it was not a "marriage of true minds" (Sonnet 116) but a straightforward business deal. Rich single women should ever keep Katherine in mind and ask themselves of their suitors: Are they wooing or dealing?

Meetings and Confrontations

When two people in an organization don't work well together, a standard solution is to arrange a meeting where they can confront each other with their interpersonal difficulties. Shakespeare was well acquainted with such meetings. After all, a battle is the ultimate confrontation between foes, and Shakespearean plays are full of fights of every size and kind. But fights aside, Shakespeare offers much advice for those who would attend a confrontation meeting. One approach is conciliatory, as when Antony, in *Antony and Cleopatra* (Act I, scene i) says: "Let's not confound the time with conference harsh."

For those who take a more aggressive tack, there is the advice Sir Toby Belch gives to the cowardly Sir Andrew Aguecheek in *Twelfth Night* (Act III, scene iv) on how to approach a gentleman with whom he has a disagreement:

> So soon as ever thou seest him, draw [a sword], and
> as thou drawest, swear horrible; for it comes to pass
> oft that a terrible oath, with a swaggering accent
> sharply twang'd off, gives manhood more
> approbation than ever proof [trial] itself would
> have earn'd him.

Sometimes bluster alone is not enough and a combination of bluster and greater abuse is appropriate. For example, in *Richard II* (Act III, scene iii) Henry Bolingbroke (later to be King Henry IV) expounds on how he will meet with King Richard, whose crown he will eventually usurp:

> Methinks King Richard and myself should meet
> With no less terror than the elements
> Of fire and water, when their thund'ring shock

At meeting tears the cloudy cheeks of heaven.
Be he the fire, I'll be the yielding water;
The rage be his, whilst on the earth I rain
My waters—on the earth, and not on him.

This is a wonderfully comic bit because "rain my waters" means "make water" or "pass water." We know this because of the pause before he catches himself and says "on the earth, and not on him." Shakespeare knew that one must always respect the office, if not the individual who temporarily occupies it—and that one should not piss off an organizational rival before he or she is powerless to retaliate.

At the end of many meetings there is a common problem of scheduling the next one. The next time you are in such a situation, all attendees with their calendars open, calling out dates to each other, think of the witches in *Macbeth* (Act I, scene i), who are in a similar scheduling dilemma:

FIRST WITCH:	When shall we three meet again
	In thunder, lightning, or in rain?
SECOND WITCH:	When the hurlyburly's done,
	When the battle's lost and won.
THIRD WITCH:	That will be ere the set of sun.
FIRST WITCH:	Where the place?
SECOND WITCH:	Upon the heath.
THIRD WITCH:	There to meet with Macbeth.

Mergers and Acquisitions

The 1980s were a time of acceleration for corporate mergers and leveraged buyouts. Shakespeare would not have been surprised by the techniques used by the merger and acquisition makers of our day. That big companies should swallow up little companies would seem as natural to him as the fish in the sea. In *Pericles* (Act II, scene i) he compares "rich misers" to whales who, if left unchecked, would swallow up a "whole parish" including the "church, steeple, bells, and all."

THIRD FISHERMAN: Master, I marvel how the fishes live in the sea.

FIRST FISHERMAN: Why, as men do a-land; the great ones eat up the little ones. I can compare our rich misers to nothing so fitly as to a whale; 'a plays and tumbles, driving the poor fry before him, and at last devours them at a mouthful. Such whales have I heard on a' th' land, who never leave gaping till they swallow'd the whole parish, church, steeple, bells, and all.

Yet Shakespeare must have believed in government regulation to maintain orderly markets so that no one whale could swallow "the whole parish." A major theme of many of his plays—the central theme in *Macbeth* and *Richard III,* for example—has a "whale" trying to illegitimately monopolize all power (or markets). When this happened in the United States, antitrust laws were enacted to restore the competitive equilibrium. Shakespeare was a great believer in having the legitimate forces of government intervene to defeat power grabs by the greedy. He knew that not even the whales (big business) could long thrive if they ate up all the small fry (small business). As he has Isabella say in *Measure for Measure* (Act II, scene ii):

> O, it is excellent
> To have a giant's strength; but it is tyrannous
> To use it like a giant.

Not only because it is not ethical, but because then you will encourage all the small fry to gang up on you.

Motivating Employees

One of the most critical tasks of any manager is motivating his or her workforce to produce a maximum effort. Sometimes this can be done by mutual cooperation. The traditional hostility and contention between labor and management is being increasingly abated by various programs of participative management. Such efforts, also known as industrial democracy, encourage joint problem solving and decision making, which in turn lead to greater harmony between workers and leaders. Yet Shakespeare knew that such cooperative efforts would bear motivational fruit. Edgar in *King Lear* (Act III, scene vi) observes that life is easier when "our betters" share "our woes":

> When we our betters see bearing our woes,
> We scarcely think our miseries our foes.
> Who alone suffers, suffers most i' the mind,
> Leaving free things and happy shows behind,
> But then the mind much sufferance doth o'erskip,
> When grief hath mates, and bearing fellowship.
> How light and portable my pain seems now,
> When that which makes me bend makes the King bow.

Another motivational technique is to distract the workers from their problems. Give them company picnics or organizational bowling leagues, or send them to night-school courses—anything to keep their minds busy so that discontent doesn't fester. This is exactly the advice the dying King Henry IV gives to his son, the Prince of Wales, in *Henry IV, Part II* (Act IV, scene v):

> Be it thy course to busy giddy minds
> With foreign quarrels, that action, hence borne out,
> May waste the memory of the former days.

The son, as King Henry V, takes over his father's job and immediately follows his advice about "foreign quarrels" by going to war with France. In *Henry V,* after his soldiers have been rebuffed during an attack on a French fort, King Henry (Act III, scene i) rallies them to another attack and victory with one of the greatest motivational speeches of all time:

Once more unto the breach, dear friends, once more;
Or close the wall up with our English dead.
In peace there's nothing so becomes a man
As modest stillness and humility;
But when the blast of war blows in our ears,
Then imitate the action of the tiger;
Stiffen the sinews, conjure up the blood,
Disguise fair nature with hard-favor'd rage;
Then lend the eye a terrible aspect;...
Now set the teeth and stretch the nostril wide,
Hold hard the breath, and bend up every spirit
To his full height. On, on, you noblest English,
Whose blood is fet [derived] from fathers of war-proof!
Fathers that, like so many Alexanders,
Have in these parts from morn till even fought
And sheath'd their swords for lack of argument.
Dishonor not your mothers; now attest
That those whom you call'd fathers did beget you.
Be copy now to men of grosser blood,
And teach them how to war. And you, good yeomen,
Whose limbs were made in England, show us here
The mettle of your pasture; let us swear

That you are worth your breeding, which I doubt not;
For there is none of you so mean and base
That hath not noble lustre in your eyes.
I see you stand like greyhounds in the slips,
Straining upon the start. The game's afoot!
Follow your spirit; and upon this charge
Cry, "God for Harry, England, and Saint George!"

Today Henry V could be called a practitioner of the path-goal leadership style, in which the leader indicates to followers the strategy ("unto the breach") with which they can accomplish a mission. With an updating of this speech's diction, any football coach giving a half-time speech in the locker room or any sales manager addressing customer representatives could use it. Remember King Henry's cry that "the game's afoot" the next time you hear someone talk of a game plan in a business meeting.

Murphy's Law

Legend has it that it was United States Air Force Captain Edsel Murphy who in 1949 first put forth the famous law: "If anything can go wrong, it will." Yet in *Henry IV, Part II* (Act IV, scene iv) Shakespeare anticipated Murphy by several centuries when he had the king ask:

> Will Fortune never come with both hands full,
> But write her fair words still in foulest terms?
> She either gives a stomach and no food—
> Such are the poor, in health; or else a feast
> And takes away the stomach—such are the rich,
> That have abundance and enjoy it not.

King Claudius observed in *Hamlet* (Act IV, scene v):

> When sorrows come, they come not single spies,
> But in battalions.

He should know. As the murderer of Hamlet's father he was the cause of most of the sorrow in the play.

Music and Productivity

Shakespeare knew the importance of music. While his plays are not musicals, many of them contain songs (which he wrote) and many others have obvious occasions for musicality. He frequently used musical analogies; King Richard in *Richard II* (Act V, scene v) observes:

> How sour sweet music is
> When time is broke, and no proportion kept!
> So is it in the music of men's lives.

Shakespeare was very aware of the relationship between music and mood. He knew that music could alter moods or perceptions, as the duke in *Measure for Measure* (Act IV, scene i) asserts:

> music oft hath such a charm
> To make bad good, and good provoke to harm.

Thus Shakespeare would not have been surprised had he been around in the 1930s to see employers first using music in the workplace to sooth tensions and thus increase productivity. Shakespeare knew music could "for the time" change nature. In *The Merchant of Venice* (Act V, scene i) Lorenzo says that there is no one

> so stockish, hard, and full of rage,
> But music for the time doth change his nature.

The man that hath no music in himself,
Nor is not moved with concord of sweet
   sounds,
Is fit for treasons, stratagems, and spoils;
The motions of his spirit are dull as night,
And his affections [inclinations] dark as
   Erebus [hell]:
Let no such man be trusted.

Shakespeare even speculated on why music was invented in the first place. Obviously looking at this from a management perspective, Lucentio in *The Taming of the Shrew* (Act III, scene i) explains

            the cause why music was ordain'd!
Was it not to refresh the mind of man
After his studies or his usual pain [labor]?

Wait, you say! Where is the famous line about how

Music hath charms to soothe the savage beast,
To soften rocks, or bend a knotted oak.

William Congreve, not Shakespeare, wrote this, in his 1697 play, *The Mourning Bride*. It just goes to show that not even Shakespeare was able to write every line people often think he did.

Negotiating Techniques

Shakespeare wrote often of sales techniques. There isn't much the modern world could have taught the Elizabethans about the psychology of the marketplace. They knew, as Berowne says in *Love's Labor's Lost* (Act IV, scene iii), that "to things of sale a seller's praise belongs." In *Henry IV, Part I* (Act III, scene i) Hotspur makes the now classic statement on the depth of bargaining:

> But in the way of bargain, mark ye me,
> I'll cavil [argue] on the ninth part of a hair.

In *Troilus and Cressida* (Act IV, scene i) Paris discusses a common tactic used by those negotiating a purchase price:

> you do as chapmen [merchants] do,
> Dispraise the thing that you desire to buy.

In the same play Shakespeare shows that selling techniques, while they vary with the times, have some aspects, such as bait and switch, that are eternal. Ulysses (Act I, scene iii) describes one of the oldest marketing stratagems:

> Let us, like merchants first show foul wares,
> And think perchance they'll sell; if not,
> The lustre of the better shall exceed,
> By showing the worse first.

A seller with all his or her wares on display could have the wind taken out of a presentation if a potential buyer suddenly says, as Rosalind did in *As You Like It* (Act III, scene v):

> For I must tell you friendly in your ear,
> Sell when you can, you are not for all markets.

As for having people bargain on your behalf, in *Much Ado About Nothing* (Act II, scene i), Claudio advises in the context of romantic negotiations:

> Let every eye negotiate for itself,
> And trust no agent.

Of course, this does not apply to literary agents. If Shakespeare had had one of those, he might have made some real money on his plays.

New Construction

The quality of construction has been a constant concern throughout the ages. In *Hamlet* (Act V, scene i) two clowns discuss which construction techniques are best.

FIRST CLOWN: What is he that builds stronger than either
    the mason, the shipwright, or the carpenter?
SECOND CLOWN: The gallows-maker, for that outlives a
    thousand tenants.

But seriously, folks! Shakespeare was thoroughly familiar with the real problems of construction management. In
Henry IV, Part II (Act I, scene iii) Lord Bardolph (in plotting a
revolution) explains how to keep new building costs under
control:

> When we mean to build,
> We first survey the plot, then draw the model;
> And when we see the figure of the house,
> Then must we rate the cost of the erection,
> Which if we find outweighs ability,
> What do we then but draw anew the model
> In fewer offices, or at least desist
> To build at all? Much more, in this great work,
> ...should we survey
> The plot of situation and the model,
> Consent upon a sure foundation,
> Question surveyors, know our own estate,
> How able such a work to undergo.

Anyone about to enter into negotiations with a builder
would be wise to take along this paragraph. Construction
techniques have evolved over the centuries, but the basic considerations of where, what and how much to build have not.

Always remember—if the "cost of the erection…outweighs ability," you had better "draw anew the model" with "fewer offices" or "desist to build at all."

Office Politics

Shakespeare would have been right at home with the bickering, conniving and pettiness of the modern office. Indeed, many of his plays have themes that could easily be updated to current management environments—and they have been. Gangster movies have several times borrowed the plot of *Macbeth.* The assassination in *Julius Caesar* comes to mind anytime minority stockholders unite to unceremoniously oust a long-standing chairman of the board. They may not kill him, but they destroy his power base, which, in a modern organizational sense, amounts to the same thing.

Office politics are often warlike in their intensity and tactics. All astute office infighters know that it is not wise to attack organizational rivals unless you are willing to kill them; that is, get them out of the organization so there is no possibility they could harm you in the future. Shakespeare's attitude on organizational rivalries is revealed by the Prince of Wales in *Henry IV, Part I* (Act V, scene iv) when he makes this celestial observation: "Two stars keep not their motion in one sphere." The prince was speaking of his rival for the throne of England, a rival he efficiently eliminates with his sword.

Shakespearean characters knew that it was important to kill and not merely wound a rival. This attitude is famously expressed by the title character in *Macbeth* (Act III, scene ii):

> We have scorch'd [wounded] the snake, not killed it.
> She'll close and be herself, whilest our poor malice
> Remains in danger of her former tooth.

Macbeth knew instinctively that if you don't kill "the snake" completely, it will recover and eventually bite you back. So if you are going to hurt someone, remember: Unless you get rid of her (or him), the day will come when "her former tooth" will bite you in the rear.

Of course, if you can't kill a rival with your sword, there is always your tongue. Office gossip was as deadly then as it can be now. Shakespeare's characters loved to gossip. As the king says in *King Lear* (Act V, scene iii):

> So we'll live,
> And pray, and sing, and tell old tales, and laugh
> At gilded butterflies, and hear poor rogues
> Talk of court news; and we'll talk with them too—
> Who loses and who wins; who's in, who's out—
> And take upon's [look upon] the mystery of things
> As if we were God's spies.

70

King Lear has a passive attitude toward gossip. Others are more active. Hero in *Much Ado About Nothing* (Act III, scene i) shows how to use an ill word like poison:

> I'll devise some honest slanders
> To stain my cousin with. One doth not know
> How much an ill word may empoison liking.

Certainly Iago in *Othello* is the definitive office slanderer. It is he, whose goal is to destroy Othello, who plants the lies about Othello's wife upon which the tragedy turns. Then, with great irony (Act III, scene iii), Iago warns Othello:

> O, beware, my lord, of jealousy!
> It is the green-ey'd monster which doth mock
> The meat it feeds on.

Later (Act IV, scene ii) Emilia, Iago's wife, figures out Iago's perfidy, though not knowing at this point that her husband is the "eternal villain":

> I will be hang'd if some eternal villain,
> Some busy and insinuating rogue,
> Some cogging [cheating], cozening slave,
>   to get some office,
> Have not devis'd this slander.

It just proves that Claudio in *Much Ado About Nothing* (Act II, scene i) was right when he observed:

Friendship is constant in all other things
Save in the office and affairs of love.

Organizational Behavior

Shakespeare anticipated many of the findings about human behavior in organizations that were first brought to the formal attention of management in the twentieth century. For example, in the 1940s psychologist Abraham Maslow first put forth his "needs hierarchy" by which individuals progressively reach self-fulfillment and become "all that they are capable of becoming." This theory of human motivation holds that it is all right that many individuals may never reach their goals because it is the striving, the ambition, that is paramount. Yet Shakespeare summed this all up in a single line when he had Cressida in *Troilus and Cressida* (Act I, scene ii) say: "Men prize the thing ungain'd more than it is."

Then there is J. Sterling Livingston's 1969 *Harvard Business Review* study, "Pygmalion in Management," in which he reported that management expectations of employee performance tend to become self-fulfilling prophecies. Yet Shakespeare had presented the essence of this scholarly analysis in two lines in *The Merchant of Venice* (Act III, scene iii); Shylock says to Antonio:

Thou call'dst me dog before thou hadst a cause,
But since I am a dog, beware my fangs.

Shakespeare even anticipated the work of Frederick Taylor, the "father of scientific management." Early in this century Taylor published his pioneering analyses of the best way to organize work. He wrote that jobs should be designed so that employees don't wear out too early in the day. Physical work should be structured so that it can be continued all day—steady, persistent effort being better than exhausting spurts. Yet John of Gaunt in *Richard II* (Act II, scene i) explained this very concept and thought himself "a prophet" for it:

Methinks I am a prophet new inspir'd,
And thus expiring do foretell of him:
His rash fierce blaze of riot cannot last,
For violent fires soon burn out themselves;
Small show'rs last long, but sudden storms
    are short;
He tires betimes [quickly] that spurs too fast
    betimes [early].

Many a management meeting offers a demonstration of Miles's Law (first formulated by Rufus E. Miles, Jr., in the late 1940s when he was an analyst in the Bureau of the Budget): "Where you stand depends on where you sit." Thus managers may be expected to argue for the policy position of the organizational unit they represent. Yet the essence of Miles's Law is clearly anticipated by Philip the Bastard in *King John* (Act II, scene i):

Well, whiles I am a beggar, I will rail,
And say there is no sin but to be rich;
And being rich, my virtue then shall be
To say there is no vice but beggary.
Since kings break faith upon commodity [expediency],
Gain, be my lord, for I will worship thee.

    As for people who work only for "gain," the Fool has a song about them in *King Lear* (Act II, scene iv):

That sir which serves and seeks for gain,
    And follows but for form,
Will pack when it begins to rain,
    And leave thee in the storm.

Performance Reports

Annual performance or efficiency reports are the bane of many organizations. Yet such evaluations of peers and subordinates are an everyday part of personnel management. Shakespeare has many of his characters evaluate others.

Some results are negative, as when the Duke of Albany in *King Lear* (Act IV, scene ii) tells his wife, Goneril: "You are not worth the dust which the rude wind blows in your face." Menenius in *Coriolanus* (Act II, scene i) tells Brutus: "Your abilities are too infant-like for doing much alone." Others are positive. Arguably the most famous performance evaluation in literature comes at the end of *Julius Caesar* (Act V, scene v) when Antony praises Brutus, who, having just lost a battle to Antony, has killed himself by "running on his sword":

> This was the noblest Roman of them all:
> All the conspirators [who killed Caesar], save only he,
> Did that they did in envy of great Caesar;
> He only, in a general honest thought
> And common good to all, made one of them.
> His life was gentle, and the elements
> So mix'd in him that Nature might stand up
> And say to all the world, "This was a man!"

Shakespeare even deals with the problem of how to cope with bad performance reports. Henry, Prince of Wales, will become King Henry V upon the death of his father, Henry IV. As prince he has a well-deserved reputation for being a brawling playboy constantly in the company of country wenches or known criminals. He justifies this (*Henry IV, Part I,* Act I, scene ii):

> Yet herein will I imitate the sun,
> Who doth permit the base contagious clouds

To smother up his beauty from the world,
That, when he please again to be himself,
Being wanted, he may be more wonder'd at,
By breaking through the foul and ugly mists
Of vapours that did seem to strangle him....
So, when this loose behavior I throw off
And pay the debt I never promised,
By how much better than my word I am,
By so much shall I falsify men's hopes;
And like bright metal on a sullen [dark] ground,
My reformation, glittering o'er my fault,
Shall show more goodly and attract more eyes
Than that which hath no foil [contrast] to set it off.

But once this classic underachiever has taken on the new job of king, he declares himself reformed and renounces old habits (*Henry IV, Part II,* Act V, scene ii):

My father is gone wild into his grave;
For in his tomb lie my affections [old wild ways],
And with his spirits sadly I survive,
To mock the expectation of the world,
To frustrate prophecies, and to rase out [erase]
Rotten opinion, who hath writ me down
After my seeming.

Then he renounces his old friends (Act V, scene v):

Presume not that I am the thing I was,
For God doth know, so shall the world perceive,

That I have turn'd away my former self;
So will I those that kept me company.

Of course, this tactic of simply dismissing past poor performance reports only works if you already have your next job. Unfortunately, a career strategy of raising hell while waiting for your father to die so that you can inherit the family business isn't available to many.

Personal Finance

Many of Shakespeare's characters were incorrigible spendthrifts, constantly complaining about borrowing and debt. Others took a very conservative attitude toward personal finance. For example, Polonius in *Hamlet* (Act I, scene iii) advises his son, Laertes:

Neither a borrower nor a lender be,
For loan oft loses both itself and friend,
And borrowing dulleth th' edge of husbandry.

And what happens when the borrower or lender gets "dull" through age or infirmity? Shakespeare recognized the necessity of fiduciary relationships in such cases. For example, in *King Lear* (Act I, scene ii) Edmund states:

> I have heard him oft maintain it to be fit that, sons
> at perfect age and fathers declin'd, the father
> should be as ward to the son, and the son manage
> his revenue.

Certainly the most outrageous borrower in all of Shakespeare is Sir John Falstaff. In *Henry IV, Part I* (Act III, scene iii) this famously fat knight offers his personal financial history tied up in a description of himself.

> I was as virtuously given as a gentleman need to be,
> virtuous enough: swore little, dic'd not above seven
> times—a week, went to a bawdy-house not above
> once in a quarter—of an hour, paid money that I
> borrow'd—three or four times, liv'd well and in
> good compass; and now I live out of all order, out
> of all compass [moderation].

When the Prince of Wales later in this same scene announces that he has "paid back" one of Sir John's debts, Falstaff complains: "O, I do not like that paying back, 'tis a double labor." By the second part of *Henry IV* (Act I, scene ii) Falstaff, still in debt, finally admits:

79

I can get no remedy against this consumption of
the purse; borrowing only liners and lingers it out,
but the disease is incurable.

Bad debts were as much a problem in Shakespeare's time
as today. For example, in *Timon of Athens* (Act II, scene ii)
Timon complains:

How goes the world, that I am thus encount'red
With clamorous demands of debt, broken bonds,
And the detention of long since due debts...?

In the Elizabethan age, as now, the forgiveness of bad
debts was often at issue. Certainly the most famous request
for mercy in this context comes in *The Merchant of Venice* (Act
IV, scene i) when Portia, acting as an attorney, asks Shylock to
forgive a debt he is owed. When he asks, "On what compul-
sion must I?" she responds:

The quality of mercy is not strain'd [forced],
It droppeth as the gentle rain from heaven
Upon the place beneath. It is twice blest:
It blesseth him that gives and him that takes.

Shakespeare knew that regardless of how tangled financial relationships became, one thing was certain, as Stephano
states in *The Tempest* (Act III, scene ii): "He that dies pays all
debts." Only then will a mortgage company show a "quality of
mercy" and forgive the debtor—because it knows that it will
eventually get its money from the estate of the deceased.

Personnel Management

Shakespeare was quite aware of many of the problems that supervisors and personnel managers face in large organizations. For instance, it is often difficult to make choices from among a group of poor job applicants. As Hortensio says in *The Taming of the Shrew* (Act I, scene i): "There's small choice in rotten apples." But even if the potential employees (or apples) look good, it is still difficult to make valid on-the-spot judgments; Imogen says in *Cymbeline* (Act IV, scene ii): "Our very eyes are sometimes like our judgments, blind." Shakespeare's characters knew that it was always difficult at best to predict on-the-job performance. Thus Banquo asks the witches in *Macbeth* (Act I, scene iii) if they can forecast whether Macbeth is in line for a promotion:

> If you can look into the seeds of time,
> And say which grain will grow, and which will not,
> Speak then to me, who neither beg nor fear
> Your favors nor your hate.

The witches respond much like management consultants—in language so obtuse that he can't figure out what it means.

The question of who you hire is answered by a court gossip known as the First Gentleman in *Henry VIII* (Act II, scene i) when he observes:

81

> This is noted,
> And generally, whoever the King favors,
> The Card'nal will instantly find employment.

Then as now there was nothing like an "in" at court. It is as Shallow, a "country justice," says in *Henry IV, Part II* (Act V, scene i): "A friend i' th' court is better than a penny in purse."

Modern job design experts seek to create positions that employees find intrinsically self-fulfilling. As Antony says in *Antony and Cleopatra* (Act IV, scene iv):

> To business that we love we rise betime,
> And go to't with delight.

Iago, in *Othello* (Act II, scene iii), knew that "pleasure and action make the hours seem short." The essence of modern job design philosophy is perhaps best summed up by Tranio in *The Taming of the Shrew* (Act I, scene i):

> No profit grows where is no pleasure ta'en.
> In brief, sir, study what you most affect [find pleasing].

Very often the personnel policies of large organizations are dysfunctional—their rigid rules often defeat their own purposes. Talented employees are often inadequately rewarded and quit as a result. Only then is it realized how valuable they were, because it proves so difficult to replace them. In *Much Ado About Nothing* (Act IV, scene i) Friar Francis observes this same problem:

               it so falls out
That what we have we prize not to the worth
Whiles we enjoy it, but being lack'd and lost,
Why then we rack the value; then we find
The virtue that possession would not show us
Whiles it was ours.

One of the most difficult aspects of personnel management is firing people. It's even worse if you are the one losing the job. Being fired in an organizational context parallels being killed in a battle. The same considerations often apply. One takes risk to achieve gain. If you are defeated in battle, you lose your life; if you are defeated in an organizational war, you often lose your job. Those who constantly worry about such losses tend to be less effective in battle or business than those who are like Caesar in *Julius Caesar* (Act II, scene ii) and can philosophically accept their eventual death (or firing):

Cowards die many times before their deaths,
The valiant never taste of death but once.
Of all the wonders that I yet have heard,
It seems to me most strange that men should fear,
Seeing that death, a necessary end,
Will come when it will come.

It was only in this century that the rejuvenating value of vacations and rest breaks was established and they were made common personnel management practices. Yet in *Henry IV, Part I* (Act I, scene ii) Prince Hal observes:

83

If all the year were playing holidays,
To sport would be as tedious as to work;
But when they seldom come, they wish'd for come,
And nothing pleaseth but rare accidents [events].

It is ironic that these lines are spoken by Prince Hal, the playboy Prince of Wales whose life to date had been lived as one long vacation. Western literature's most famous low achiever proves the point that long vacations can be beneficial. After all, almost as soon as Prince Hal's "vacation" is over, he shows that it prepared him to conquer France. Talk about effective sabbaticals!

Planning

Shakespeare understood how critical careful planning is to any enterprise. On the evening before the great Battle of Bosworth Field, King Richard in *Richard III* (Act V, scene iii) explains how he will develop a staffing plan for the next day's work.

Give me some ink and paper in my tent;
I'll draw the form and model of our battle,
Limit [appoint] each leader to his several charge,
And part in just proportion our small power.

It is easy to plan for something that is certain to come, like a battle, compared to planning in uncertainty. Cassius in *Julius Caesar* (Act V, scene i) explains the philosophy behind the concept of contingency planning:

> But since the affairs of men rests still uncertain,
> Let's reason with the worst that may befall.

Cassius would fit in with any modern staff trying to antici-pate Murphy's Law by developing and planning for worst-case scenarios—for when anything that can, will go wrong. Brutus, in that same scene, offers quite a contrast. He com-plains about working in a state of uncertainty and expresses a universal longing to know how things will turn out in the end.

> O that a man might know
> The end of this day's business ere it come!
> But it sufficeth that the day will end,
> And then the end is known.

Plans are comparatively easy enough to make. What is hard is getting other people to carry them out. The conspira-tors who assassinated Caesar had this same problem. In the following dialogue from *Julius Caesar* (Act II, scene i) they consider inviting Cicero, the famous Roman orator, to join them because "his silver hairs" will help sell their cause.

CASSIUS: But what of Cicero? Shall we sound him?
              I think he will stand very strong with us.
CASCA: Let us not leave him out.
CINNA: No, by no means.
METELLUS: O, let us have him, for his silver hairs
              Will purchase us a good opinion,
              And buy men's voices to commend our deeds.
              It shall be said his judgment rul'd our hands;
              Our youths and wildness shall no whit appear,
              But all be buried in his gravity.
BRUTUS: O, name him not; let us not break with [reveal
                our secret to] him,
              For he will never follow any thing
              That other men begin.
CASSIUS: Then leave him out.
CASCA: Indeed he is not fit.

Note that on Brutus' advice they reject Cicero because he is a very common management type—the person who won't follow plans made by others. It is just as Alexander Hamilton, President George Washington's secretary of the treasury and the man who wrote the first economic plan for the United States, said in *The Federalist Papers* (no. 70, 1788): "Men often oppose a thing merely because they have had no agency in planning it, or because it may have been planned by those whom they dislike." Both Shakespeare and the man on the ten-dollar bill knew that some people who are great leaders or orators cannot be trusted to be followers—and you can plan on that!

Policy Analysis

Shakespeare could conceptualize the essence of policy analysis as well as any modern MBA. He knew that a rigorous policy analysis had to face facts without flinching at their consequences. Thus in *Timon of Athens* (Act III, scene ii) he has the First Stranger observe:

> But I perceive
> Men must learn now with pity to dispense,
> For policy sits above conscience.

No policy "dispenses" more "with pity" than war. In *Henry IV, Part II* (Act IV, scene i) the Archbishop of York presents his analysis of why war is a justifiable policy:

> I have in equal balance justly weigh'd
> What wrongs our arms may do, what wrongs we suffer,
> And find our griefs [grievances] heavier than our
>   offenses.

Policy decisions often turn on estimates of the costs involved. In *The Merchant of Venice* (Act I, scene i) Bassanio insults Gratiano with this classic benefit-cost analysis:

> Gratiano speaks an infinite deal of nothing, more
> than any man in all Venice. His reasons are as two
> grains of wheat hid in two bushels of chaff; you
> shall seek all day ere you find them, and when you
> have them, they are not worth the search.

Shakespeare also knew how to assess the utility of a policy decision that turns out to be a mistake. Such a decision should not necessarily be reversed, if a point of no return has been reached; that is, if it is no more costly to go on than to reverse. Macbeth in *Macbeth* (Act III, scene iv) arrives at just this policy analysis after he has embarked on his series of murders:

> I am in blood
> Stepp'd in so far that, should I wade no more,
> Returning were as tedious as go o'er.

Here we have Macbeth analyzing his sunk costs and realizing that he has invested so much in murder that he might as well continue with that policy.

Often policymakers analyze a situation and find themselves paralyzed by doubt. It is as Lucio says in *Measure for Measure* (Act I, scene iv):

> Our doubts are traitors,
> And make us lose the good we oft might win
> By fearing to attempt.

Certainly the one character in all of Shakespeare's plays who is most famous for being wracked by doubt and indecision is Hamlet, the Prince of Denmark, who takes a seemingly interminable time deciding whether to kill himself or his uncle Claudius (the current king), who murdered his father (the previous king). In *Hamlet* (Act III, scene i) he analyzes indecisiveness toward the end of his famous "to be, or not to be" soliloquy. He finds, as has been subsequently verified, that too much thinking, "the pale cast of thought," often leads only to inaction:

> Thus conscience does make cowards of us all;
> And thus the native hue of resolution
> Is sicklied o'er with the pale cast of thought,
> And enterprises of great pitch and moment
> With this regard their currents turn awry,
> And lose the name of action.

Had Hamlet not been the boss's son (later the boss's nephew as well as the boss's wife's son), his constant introspection and inability to finish what he started would have gotten him fired from any number of prince trainee positions.

Portfolio Theory

One of the most basic principles of investing is diversification: "Don't put all your eggs in one basket." Indeed, the 1990 Nobel Prize in economics was awarded to several American business school professors who used mathematical models to illustrate modern "portfolio theory." But their conclusions were in essence no different than what Shakespeare so obviously stated more than 400 years ago. In *The Merchant of Venice* (Act I, scene i) Antonio (a Venetian merchant) sums the theory up in four lines:

> My ventures are not in one bottom [ship] trusted,
> Nor to one place; nor is my whole estate
> Upon the fortune of the present year:
> Therefore my merchandise makes me not sad.

Antonio has well positioned his assets to survive a reversal of fortune. His goods are in multiple ships bound to multiple ports. Additionally, he has a reserve that is not at risk during the current year. Thus he can recover even if some of his ships are sunk and some of his merchandise lost. His counterpart today would have assets invested in stocks, gold, real estate, corporate bonds and government bonds. One way or the other, Antonio thinks, he will financially survive any possible hard times. Thus we can conclude that Shakespeare's analysis of portfolio theory was included in his First Folio collection of plays—published in 1623.

Pound of Flesh

Because Shakespeare was himself a very successful businessman, he was necessarily well acquainted with all aspects of business law—especially the law of contracts. He knew that sudden or unadvised contracts should be avoided; Juliet in *Romeo and Juliet* (Act II, scene ii) complains of the "too rash" contract she makes with Romeo:

> I have no joy of this contract to-night,
> It is too rash, too unadvis'd, too sudden,
> Too like the lightning, which doth cease to be
> Ere one can say it lightens.

Certainly the most famous business contract dispute in Western literature is Shylock's attempt in *The Merchant of Venice* (Act IV, scene i) to get a court to enforce his contract for "a pound of flesh"—now the classic description for any exceedingly harsh demand. When Antonio borrowed money from Shylock, he signed a contract agreeing to pay a pound of his flesh upon default. Circumstances force him into default, and Shylock sues. The rest of the play is a demonstration of the legal maxim that no contract was ever written that couldn't be broken. In the climactic courtroom scene, Bassanio (Antonio's friend) begs the court to allow the bond to be paid "ten times o'er" instead of taking the "pound of flesh," which is now legally due. He pleads: "To do a great right, do a little wrong." The play then turns on the legal brilliance of a young woman named Portia. Disguising herself as a male lawyer, she appears for the defense. There follows this classic courtroom surprise.

PORTIA: A pound of that same merchant's flesh is thine,
           The court awards it, and the law doth give it....
           And you must cut this flesh from off his
               breast....
SHYLOCK: Most learned judge, a sentence! Come prepare!
           [This is when the actor playing Shylock
               traditionally and conspicuously sharpens his
               knife.]
PORTIA: Tarry a little, there is something else.
           This bond doth give thee here no jot of blood;
           The words expressly are "a pound of flesh."
           Take then thy bond, take thou thy pound of
               flesh,
           But in the cutting it, if thou dost shed
           One drop of Christian blood, thy lands and
               goods
           Are by the laws of Venice confiscate
           Unto the state of Venice....
SHYLOCK: Is that the law?
PORTIA: Thyself shalt see the act;
           For as thou urgest justice, be assur'd
           Thou shalt have justice more than thou
               desir'st...
SHYLOCK: I take this offer, then; pay the bond thrice
           And let the Christian go.
BASSANIO: Here is the money.

PORTIA: Soft,
    The Jew shall have all justice. Soft, no haste.
    He shall have nothing but the penalty....
    Therefore prepare thee to cut off the flesh.
    Shed thou no blood, nor cut thou less nor more
    But just a pound a flesh. If thou tak'st more
    Or less than a just pound, be it but so much
    As makes it light or heavy in the substance
    Or the division of the twenti[e]th part
    Of one poor scruple, nay, if the scale do turn
    But in the estimation of a hair,
    Thou diest, and all thy goods are confiscate.

There is no better example of breaking an otherwise valid contract. This scene is so famous that *Portia* has become an eponym for a female lawyer. But there is one thing about this famous fictional case that most people don't realize because they have been so absorbed by the high drama of the legal legerdemain—*The Merchant of Venice* is one of Shakespeare's comedies.

Practicing Business Ethics

P. T. Barnum (1810–1891) is credited with observing that "there's a sucker born every minute," meaning that there is an almost limitless supply of people ready to be duped. But that idea was around at least as early as the sixteenth century. Iago, the villain in *Othello*, remarks (Act I, scene iii) that the Moor of Venice, Othello himself, is one of these "suckers":

> The Moor is of a free and open nature,
> That thinks men honest that but seem to be so,
> And will as tenderly be led by th' nose
> As asses are.

Many of Shakespeare's characters, like Iago, had a tenuous relationship to business ethics. As Autolycus, a peddler, says in *The Winter's Tale* (Act IV, scene iv): "Though I am not naturally honest, I am so sometimes by chance." The classic justification for unethical behavior—that everybody does it—comes from *Timon of Athens*; Timon (Act IV, scene iii) explains how "each thing's a thief."

> I'll example you with thievery:
> The sun's a thief, and with his great attraction
> Robs the vast sea; the moon's an arrant thief,
> And her pale fire she snatches from the sun;
> The sea's a thief, whose liquid surge resolves [melts]
> The moon into salt tears; the earth's a thief,
> That feeds and breeds by a composture [manure] stol'n

From gen'ral excrement; each thing's a thief.
The laws, your curb and whip, in their rough power
   [unjust law],
Has uncheck'd theft.

Trust and integrity are critical in business. Even in this age of lawyers when written contracts abound, much of everyday business is based upon the word of one person to another. Thus, once one's reputation for integrity is lost, one's effectiveness is also lost. Polonius offers this advice to his son, Laertes, in *Hamlet* (Act I, scene iii).

This above all: to thine own self be true,
And it must follow, as the night the day,
Thou canst not then be false to any man.

Ironically, Polonius doesn't follow this advice himself. He is that typical business hypocrite who advises people to act not as he does, but as he says. He advises his son to "be true" but tells his daughter to appear more pious than she really is, and he himself eavesdrops on the royal family by hiding behind curtains. This last indiscretion leads to his death.

Yet Polonius' hypocrisy is nothing compared to the outright devilishness of Richard III. In *Henry VI, Part III* the Duke of Gloucester (later to be Richard III) seeks to set new standards for double-dealing dishonest actions. He lies and murders his way to the English throne, all the while keeping the audience informed of his plans via soliloquies such as this (Act III, scene ii):

> I'll play the orator as well as Nestor,
> Deceive more slily than Ulysses could,
> And like a Sinon, take another Troy.
> I can add colors to the chameleon,
> Change shapes with Proteus for advantages,
> And set the murtherous Machevil to school.

Gloucester uses imagery from Homer's *Iliad* to illustrate his wickedness: Nestor was the Greeks' greatest orator, Ulysses their greatest schemer and Sinon the great liar who convinced the Trojans to bring the wooden horse within their walls. Proteus was a Greek god who could assume different shapes. And Machevil (Niccolo Machiavelli) was the most evil man in Renaissance letters. Teaching him new tricks ("set...to school") was bad indeed. Gloucester then concludes by asking:

> Can I do this, and cannot get a crown?
> Tut, were it farther off, I'll pluck it down.

This man will do anything to achieve success, including murdering all the people whose lives stand between him and his coronation as king of England. His obsession to succeed differs only in degree from that of some modern business competitors.

Perhaps the most eloquent defense of unethical behavior in all of Shakespeare is Sir John Falstaff's justification to himself in *Henry IV, Part I* of why he does not do the honorable thing and participate in the battle then raging. At first

(Act V, scene i) he concludes that "honor pricks me on," but then reconsiders:

> Yea, but how if honor prick me off when I come on? how then? Can honor set to a leg? No. Or an arm? No. Or take away the grief of a wound? No. Honor hath no skill in surgery then? No. What is honor? A word. What is in that word honor? What. is that honor? Air. A trim reckoning! Who hath it? He that died a' Wednesday. Doth he feel it? No. Doth he hear it? No. 'Tis insensible, then?: Yea, to the dead. But will't not live with the living? No. Why? Detraction will not suffer it. Therefore I'll none of it, honor is a mere scutcheon [shield on a coat of arms]. And so ends my catechism.

Later, after pretending to be dead on the field of battle to avoid having to fight, Falstaff concludes (Act V, scene iv):

> The better part of valor is discretion, in the which better part I have sav'd my life.

This most famous justification for cowardice and dishonesty is often misquoted as "discretion is the better part of valor." But there was nothing of valor or honesty in Falstaff's actions. Yet this professional petty thief remains one of the most beloved characters in all of Shakespeare—perhaps because so many people identify with him and sympathize with his dishonesty. Prince Hamlet said in *Hamlet* (Act II, scene ii) that "to be honest, as this world goes, is to be one man pick'd out of ten thousand." Falstaff certainly wasn't that "one man." Are you?

Presentation Techniques

A formal presentation often makes or breaks a business deal. The long-winded, pompous courtier Polonius in *Hamlet* (Act II, scene ii) delivers this most famous statement on the length of speeches:

> Therefore, since brevity is the soul of wit,
> And tediousness the limbs and outward flourishes,
> I will be brief.

The statement is ironic since Polonius is anything but brief on anything. If he had appeared in *Hamlet*, Holofernes from *Love's Labor's Lost* (Act V, scene i) would have certainly said of him, "He draweth out the thread of his verbosity finer than the staple of his argument." Queen Gertrude in *Hamlet*, being on the receiving end of Polonius' verbosity, shows her annoyance with him (Act II, scene ii) when she delivers this famous put-down of all windy speeches: "More matter, with less art."

The inability to make an appropriate presentation is often fatal to executive careers. When, in *King Lear*, Lear's daughter Cordelia cannot express her affection for her father to his satisfaction, he warns her (Act I, scene i):

> Mend your speech a little,
> Lest you may mar your fortunes.

Because she is unable to make an appropriately fawning speech, she is disinherited by a father who cannot tolerate a reluctant flatterer.

A common technique for gaining an audience's sympathy is to present yourself as an amateur speaker. This allows you, if you are indeed a gifted speaker, to sneak up on the audience's emotions, exactly as Antony does in *Julius Caesar* (Act III, scene ii) at Caesar's funeral. First he denies that he is about to make an emotional appeal, then he denies that he is an orator, but he goes on to make one of the most powerful orations ever to "stir men's blood":

> I come not, friends, to steal away your hearts.
> I am no orator, as Brutus is;
> But (as you know me all) a plain blunt man
> That love my friend, and that they know full well
> That gave me public leave to speak of him.
> For I have neither wit, nor words, nor worth,
> Action, nor utterance, nor the power of speech
> To stir men's blood; I only speak right on...

Antony's last phrase achieved a great revival in the 1960s when many a student demonstration was punctuated by cries of "Right on!"

But *Hamlet* (Act III, scene ii) offers Shakespeare's greatest advice on public speaking. Hamlet advises some actors preparing to perform the play-within-a-play that he has written:

> Speak the speech, I pray you, as I pronounc'd it to you, trippingly on the tongue, but if you mouth it, as many of our players do, I had as live [lief, or willingly] the town-crier spoke my lines. Nor do not saw the air too much with your hand, thus, but use all gently, for in the very torrent, tempest, and, as I may say, the whirlwind of your passion, you must acquire and beget a temperance that may give it smoothness....Be not too tame neither, but let your own discretion be your tutor. Suit the action to the word, the word to the action, with this special observance, that you o'erstep not the modesty of nature.

In this media age no executive of a major organization can afford to ignore this advice. Indeed, many, such as Lee Iacocca, Frank Perdue and Orville Redenbacher, have become media celebrities by acting (as themselves) in television commercials. Sometimes it is more important to be able to act the part than to be the part. One of the reasons often given for Ronald Reagan's success as president of the United States in the 1980s is that no matter what people thought of his policies, almost everyone agreed that he played the role very well. Reagan knew, as Shakespeare, a fellow actor, wrote in *Hamlet* (Act II, scene ii), that "the play's the thing."

Promotions

Almost everybody wants to be promoted. Personnel managers often say that the assembly-line worker who wants to be a first-line supervisor is every bit as anxious about his or her prospects as the second vice-president who wants to be a first vice-president. The job may be higher, but the level of anxiety is equal. It is as Isabella says in *Measure for Measure* (Act III, scene i):

> the poor beetle that we tread upon
> In corporal sufferance finds a pang as great
> As when a giant dies.

The problem with promotion, then as now, is judging merit. As Parolles says in *All's Well That Ends Well* (Act III, scene vi): "The merit of service is seldom attributed to the true and exact performer." Yet the Duke of Norfolk defends merit promotion in *Henry VIII* (Act I, scene i), when describing the Cardinal of York, who, "not propp'd by ancestry," uses the "force of his own merit" to buy "a place next to the King":

> There's in him stuff that puts him to these ends;
> For, being not propp'd by ancestry, whose grace
> Chalks successors their way, nor call'd upon
> For high feats done to th' crown, neither allied
> To eminent assistants, but spider-like
> Out of his self-drawing web, 'a gives us note
> The force of his own merit makes his way—
> A gift that heaven gives for him, which buys
> A place next to the King.

When promotional opportunities occur in an organization, the question often arises whether to select a replacement by seniority or merit. In *Othello* (Act I, scene i) Iago vents his frustration about being passed over for promotion:

> 'Tis the curse of service,
> Preferment goes by letter and affection,
> And not by old gradation, where each second
> Stood heir to th' first.

The issue of seniority versus merit is a constant tension in organizations. Iago's bitterness, expressed here in the first act, is so great that he spends the rest of the play scheming to destroy Othello, the minority employee (he was a Moor) who denied Iago the promotion he craved.

Even in Shakespeare's day good domestic helpers were rare. In *As You Like It* (Act II, scene iii) Orlando says to Adam, an old servant:

> O good old man, how well in thee appears
> The constant service of the antique world,
> When service sweat for duty, not for meed [reward]!
> Thou art not for the fashion of these times,
> Where none will sweat but for promotion,
> And having that do choke their service up
> Even with the having. It is not so with thee.

Adam responds: "Master,...I will follow thee to the last gasp, with truth and loyalty." You just can't find workers like that anymore! But just as Orlando says, you couldn't then, either. His basic complaint is that "none will sweat but for promotion." Some things never change!

Of course, the best way to gain a promotion without having to sweat for it is to be fortunate enough to be in the right place at the right time. As Malvolio states in *Twelfth Night* (Act II, scene v): "Be not afraid of greatness. Some are born great, some achieve greatness, and some have greatness thrust upon 'em." But waiting to "have greatness thrust upon" you is playing against the odds. Shakespeare knew, as Constance states in *King John* (Act III, scene i), that "that strumpet Fortune" was not to be trusted.

Psychic Income

One of the most difficult things to accomplish in any large organization is instilling an equitable system of rewards. In *Hamlet* the prince discusses with Polonius, the lord chamberlain (or chief administrator) of the Danish royal court, what to pay a band of visiting players; Polonius in his role as a financial officer suggests that they be paid "according to their desert." But Prince Hamlet (Act II, scene ii) disagrees. We know he has just returned from college, and we may now surmise that he has been studying wage and salary administration, because he recommends that the players should be well paid in spite of how deserving they are.

POLONIUS: My lord, I will use them according to their desert.

HAMLET: God's bodkin, man, much better: use every man after his desert, and who shall scape whipping? Use them after your own honor and dignity—the less they deserve, the more merit is in your bounty.

But all good managers know that it is not enough just to pay employees with money. Even the best workers need a certain amount of psychological stroking; they need to be praised and made to feel appreciated. In *The Winter's Tale* (Act I, scene ii) Hermione notes:

> One good deed dying tongueless
> Slaughters a thousand waiting upon that.
> Our praises are our wages.

Today this is known as psychic income, then as now the most naturally plentiful thing you can give any employee—and cheap, too.

Shakespeare, the managerial psychologist, knew that changing the name of a thing could immediately change its value. In a great comic bit in *Love's Labor's Lost* (Act III, scene i), Costard expounds how it's better to be paid a "remuneration" than mere money:

> Now will I look to his remuneration.
> Remuneration! O, that's the Latin word for three
> farthings: three farthings—remuneration.—
> "What's the price of this inkle?"—"One penny."—
> "No, I'll give you a remuneration": why, it carries it.
> Remuneration: why, it is a fairer name than French
> crown! I will never buy and sell out of this word.

This is the same logic that makes sophisticated managers eschew formal job description titles for informal working titles. Thus a senior clerk-stenographer is happier being an "office manager," just as the accountant IV prefers to be the "chief accountant." But in one instance it must be admitted that Shakespeare got it wrong. He had Juliet say in *Romeo and Juliet* (Act II, scene ii):

> that which we call a rose
> By any other name would smell as sweet.

Juliet was mistaken, because some roses by other names

do smell even better, just as "remuneration" sounds like a better deal than "three farthings." Of course, it's all in the head—that's why it's called psychic income.

Public Relations

All large organizations must maintain good public relations with their various "publics," whether they be employees, stockholders, customers, governments or the general public. This task often falls upon the chief executive officer. Shakespeare's plays can offer much advice to those who would practice effective public relations for their organization or cause. For example, in *Macbeth* (Act I, scene v) Lady Macbeth tells her husband as they are about to receive visitors:

> Your face, my thane, is as a book, where men
> May read strange matters. To beguile the time,
> Look like the time; bear welcome in your eye,
> Your hand, your tongue; look like th' innocent flower,
> But be the serpent under't.

One is reminded of Prince Hamlet's famous statement on facial makeovers in *Hamlet* (Act III, scene i): "God hath given you one face, and you make yourselves another." But Shakespeare went beyond makeup. He even understood the importance of body language in personal presentations. In *Troilus and Cressida* (Act IV, scene v) Ulysses describes Cressida:

> There's language in her eye, her cheek, her lip,
> Nay, her foot speaks; her wanton spirits look out
> At every joint and motive [limb] of her body.

She obviously made a good impression—through the astute use of her body language—and she was naturally good at it. Others have to work much harder to make good impressions. For two-faced posturing and effective impression management, few can top the Duke of Buckingham. In *Richard III* (Act III, scene v) he explains his skill at manipulating public perceptions:

> Tut, I can counterfeit the deep tragedian,
> Speak and look back, and pry on every side,
> Tremble and start at wagging of a straw;
> Intending [pretending] deep suspicion, ghastly looks
> Are at my service, like enforced smiles;
> And both are ready in their offices
> At any time to grace my strategems.

Then there are always those unfortunate souls who feel, warranted or not, that they have no skill at presenting themselves to the world. Such was Othello. In *Othello* (Act I, scene iii) he explains why public speaking is not his strong suit:

> Rude am I in my speech,
> And little bless'd with the soft phrase of peace;...
> And little of this great world can I speak
> More than pertains to feats of broils and battle,
> And therefore little shall I grace my cause
> In speaking for myself.

The problem is, if you don't speak for yourself, others will. And perhaps talk themselves into your job. Unless, of course, it is realized, as the First Murderer states in *Richard III* (Act I, scene iii), that "talkers are no good doers"—except in public relations, where talking is the essence of doing.

Retirement

In the Elizabethan age retirement was not a problem for the mass of the people. Most simply did not live long enough. Yet Shakespeare often dealt with the issue. Adam, in *As You Like It* (Act II, scene iii), explains to Orlando how and why he developed his personal social security system:

> I have five hundred crowns,
> The thrifty hire I sav'd under your father,
> Which I did store to be my foster-nurse
> When service should in my old limbs lie lame,
> And unregarded age in corners thrown.

At least Adam, a servant, had his savings. Old Cardinal Wolsey had all his goods confiscated when he was forcibly retired by the king. In *Henry VIII* (Act III, scene ii) he complains:

> My robe,
> And my integrity to heaven, is all
> I dare now call mine own....
> Had I but serv'd my God with half the zeal
> I serv'd my king, He would not in mine age
> Have left me naked to mine enemies.

Of course, if you knew all the nasty things Wolsey did for his king, you might well think that merely being left "naked to mine enemies" was a kindness. Justice would have warranted a retirement so quickly followed by death that he would hardly have had time to complain of it.

But even a graceful retirement from one's job is a bittersweet experience. The recognition that death is necessarily near makes many people forestall announcing their retirement, assuming they have that option, for as long as possible. Certainly the most famous announcement of retirement in Western literature is King Lear's decision in *King*

Lear (Act I, scene i) to divide his kingdom among his three children and "crawl toward death":

> 'tis our fast intent
> To shake all cares and business from our age,
> Conferring them on younger strengths, while we
> Unburthen'd crawl toward death.

This was a most unfortunate retirement decision, resulting in what has ever since been the classic example of why one should not in life assign all one's assets to one's children and thus be dependent upon their charity. Lear did just that and spent the rest of a very long play regretting it, so much so that he cursed one of his daughters (Act I, scene iv) and asked the gods to give her a "child of spleen" so

> that she may feel
> How sharper than a serpent's tooth it is
> To have a thankless child!

By the end of the play Lear and all his daughters are dead. The tragedy is that a civil war, with countless others dead as well, could have been avoided with more effective preretirement planning.

Roles and Role Models

The story goes that on being asked how to be a good actor, George Burns responded: "Always be sincere. If you can fake that, you've got it made." Shakespeare knew that the ability to fake it, or play a role, was an important skill for those who would succeed in any line of work. In *Hamlet* (Act III, scene iv) Prince Hamlet said to a person (his mother) who expressed feelings of personal inadequacy: "Assume a virtue, if you have it not." And Macbeth himself asserted in *Macbeth* (Act I, scene vii): "False face must hide what the false heart doth know."

In the twentieth century the social sciences have taught us that we all play roles in the various societies to which we belong. A considerable body of management literature analyzes these roles and their life cycles, and an equally large output of self-help works seeks to teach us how better to play our roles. All this would have been very familiar to Shakespeare, whose characters often talked self-consciously of the roles they played in life. In *Richard II* (Act V, scene v) a despondent King Richard analyzes his executive status and wishes himself "a beggar" until the idea of "crushing penury" convinces him that it's not so bad being king after all. He sounds like a depressed (which he was) senior executive who longs for the simple life on the assembly line until he thinks it through and realizes that he is so burned out that what he really wants to be is nothing. This psychological state helps explain his abdication.

Thus play I in one person many people,
And none contented. Sometimes am I king;
Then treasons make me wish myself a beggar,
And so I am. Then crushing penury
Persuades me I was better when a king,
Then am I king'd again, and by and by
Think that I am unking'd by Bullingbrook,
And straight am nothing. But what e'er I be,
Nor I, nor any man that but man is,
With nothing shall be pleas'd, till he be eas'd
With being nothing.

The best organizational role-players are always conscious of their roles and that those roles are simply roles. The clearest example of this phenomenon is an adversary proceeding of any kind. The two sides, usually lawyers, argue or fight with each other as if they hated each other's guts. But when the exercise is over there is no ill will. Shakespeare described this dynamic in *The Taming of the Shrew* (Act I, scene ii); Tranio says:

[Let's] do as adversaries do in law,
Strive mightily, but eat and drink as friends.

It is expected that one will play different roles at different times of one's management career: at first the eager management trainee, then the technical supervisor, later the middle manager, then senior manager, perhaps to the very top. Then suddenly, upon retirement, it is all gone and one is "sans every thing." Organizational careers are much like Shakespeare anticipated them to be in *As You Like It* (Act II, scene vii) when Jaques explains that "all the world's a stage." It doesn't take much of a leap of the imagination to apply his "seven ages of man" to organizational careers.

All the world's a stage,
And all the men and women merely players;
They have their exits and their entrances,
And one man in his time plays many parts,
His acts being seven ages. At first the infant,
Mewling and puking in the nurse's arms.
Then the whining schoolboy, with his satchel
And shining morning face, creeping like snail
Unwillingly to school. And then the lover,
Sighing like furnace, with a woeful ballad
Made to his mistress' eyebrow. Then a soldier,
Full of strange oaths, and bearded like the
    pard [leopard],
Jealous in honor, sudden, and quick in quarrel,
Seeking the bubble reputation
Even in the cannon's mouth. And then the justice,
In fair round belly with good capon lin'd,
With eyes severe and beard of formal cut,
Full of wise saws and modern instances;
And so he plays his part. The sixt[h] age shifts
Into the lean and slipper'd pantaloon,
With spectacles on nose, and pouch on side,
His youthful hose, well sav'd, a world too wide

For his shrunk shank, and his big manly voice,
Turning again toward childish treble, pipes
And whistles in his sound. Last scene of all,
That ends this strange eventful history,
Is second childishness, and mere oblivion,
Sans teeth, sans eyes, sans taste, sans every thing.

But how do we know what roles to play and when to play them? We learn this from role models, the people we choose to imitate. The aspiring manager will emulate the top brass, the princes of the organization. It is they, as Ophelia explains in *Hamlet* (Act III, scene i), who are

The glass of fashion and the mould of form,
Th' observ'd of all observers.

This is reinforced in Shakespeare's long poem *The Rape of Lucrece*:

For princes are the glass, the school, the book,
Where subjects' eyes do learn, do read, do look.

But whatever our aspirations may be, it is so often true that the company we keep determines how we create our roles, as Sir John Falstaff claims in *Henry IV, Part II* (Act V, scene i):

It is certain that either wise bearing or ignorant
carriage is caught, as men take diseases, one of

another; therefore let men take heed of their company.

Finally, Shakespeare took the full measure of all the roles we play. In *Macbeth* (Act V, scene v) a soliloquy by the title character seeks to put it all in perspective and answer the ultimate question: What does it all mean?

> Life's but a walking shadow, a poor player,
> That struts and frets his hour upon the stage,
> And then is heard no more. It is a tale
> Told by an idiot, full of sound and fury,
> Signifying nothing.

What Shakespeare says here about life also applies to a great deal of business activity. What with poor players, strutting and fretting and tales told by idiots, he might well be talking about the entertainment industry—perhaps daytime television.

School of Hard Knocks

Despite the easy availability of management training, many experienced executives still maintain that the best education is to be had not in the classroom but in the school of hard knocks. Shakespeare knew that life's buffeting would sometimes offer what no book learnin' could. And his characters often told of these early character-building experiences.

To attend the school of hard knocks, one first has to leave home. Petruchio explains why in *The Taming of the Shrew* (Act I, scene ii) when Hortensio asks him: "What happy gale blows you to Padua here from old Verona?"

> Such wind as scatters young men through the world
> To seek their fortunes farther than at home,
> Where small experience grows

And why leave the safety of home to risk hunger and danger in a cruel world? Because, as Regan says in *King Lear* (Act II, scene iv):

> O sir, to willful men,
> The injuries that they themselves procure
> Must be their schoolmasters.

Some of the harshest lessons in the school of hard knocks were learned by Marc Antony. In *Antony and Cleopatra* (Act I, scene iv) Octavius Caesar reminds him that as a young soldier times were very rough:

> Thou didst drink
> The stale [urine] of horses and the gilded [slimy] puddle
> Which beasts would cough at; thy palate then did deign
> The roughest berry on the rudest hedge;
> Yea, like the stag, when snow the pasture sheets,
> It is reported thou didst eat strange flesh,
> Which some did die to look on.

Was this "strange flesh" human? Shakespeare never says. But near-starvation is certainly character-building. One is reminded of Scarlett O'Hara in the middle of *Gone With the Wind* swearing to herself that she will do whatever she has to do so that she'll "never be hungry again." It gave her the motivation to succeed by whatever means necessary.

But the ultimate statement on the utility of the school of hard knocks' curriculum is made by Duke Senior in *As You Like It* (Act II, scene i) when he asserts:

> Sweet are the uses of adversity,
> Which like the toad, ugly and venomous,
> Wears yet a precious jewel in his head.

The "precious jewel" is experience. It is just this kind of experience that the Prince of Wales seeks in *Henry IV, Part II*. As the Earl of Warwick explains the situation to the king (Act IV, scene iv):

> The Prince but studies his companions
> Like a strange tongue, wherein, to gain the language,

'Tis needful that the most immodest word
Be look'd upon and learnt, which once attain'd,
Your Highness knows, comes to no further use
But to be known and hated. So, like gross terms,
The Prince will in the perfectness of time
Cast off his followers, and their memory
Shall as a pattern or a measure live,
By which his Grace must mete [appraise] the lives
    of others,
Turning past evils to advantages.

He sees that the prince, the boss's son, soon to inherit the
family business, has been hanging about with the roughnecks
and riffraff of the company so that he'll be a better supervisor of them later on. After all, the essential good of attend-
ing the school of hard knocks is to turn "past evils to
advantages."

Settling Disputes

Today there are a variety of dispute settlement techniques
short of legal action. Most involve some sort of third-party
arbitration. In Shakespeare's plays the first resort in a dispute

was often combat. In *Richard II* (Act I, scene i) the king orders two of his quarreling nobles to settle their arguments in a duel, thus letting "swords and lances arbitrate":

> We were not born to sue, but to command,
> Which since we cannot do to make you friends,
> Be ready, as your lives shall answer it,
> At Coventry upon Saint Lambert's day.
> There shall your swords and lances arbitrate
> The swelling difference of your settled hate.

Shakespeare knew—as he said in another context, "it must follow, as the night the day" (*Hamlet*, Act I, scene iii)— that peace follows war. And peace is the goal of all dispute settlements. Such a win-win process is described by the Archbishop of York in *Henry IV, Part II* (Act IV, scene ii):

> A peace is of the nature of a conquest;
> For then both parties nobly are subdued,
> And neither party loser.

In many of Shakespeare's plays, battles well belie the assertion that war never settled anything. But Shakespeare also provides (in *Coriolanus*, Act II, scene i) the following stinging denunciation by Menenius of two low-level arbitrators (judges) of ancient Rome:

> You wear out a good wholesome forenoon in
> hearing a cause between an orange-wife and a

forset-seller [seller of taps for kegs], and then rejourn [adjourn] the controversy of threepence to a second day of audience. When you are hearing a matter between party and party, if you chance to be pinch'd with the colic, you make faces like mummers [masked actors], set up the bloody flag [war banner] against all patience, and, in roaring for a chamber-pot, dismiss the controversy bleeding, the more entangled by your hearing. All the peace you make in their cause is calling both the parties knaves.

It seems that it was as true then as it is now: If your arbitrator has a bellyache, you're going to suffer as well.

Spotless Reputation

Reputation in business, whether of an individual or an organization, is a highly valued asset. Indeed, when businesses are sold they often sell for sums far in excess of their book value because of their intangible "good will" or reputation in the community. In *Henry IV, Part I* (Act I, scene ii) Sir John Falstaff bemoans the fact that both he and the young Prince of Wales have such poor reputations and states: "I would to God thou and I knew where a commodity of good names were to be bought."

Shakespeare often addressed issues of professional reputation and honor. In *Othello* (Act II, scene iii) Cassio complains:

> Reputation, reputation, reputation! O, I have lost
> my reputation! I have lost the immortal part of
> myself, and what remains is bestial.

Iago then consoles him:

> Reputation is an idle and most false imposition; oft
> got without merit, and lost without deserving.

Later (Act III, scene iii) Iago reassesses the value of reputation, posturing for Othello's benefit:

> Good name in man and woman, dear my lord,
> Is the immediate jewel of their souls.
> Who steals my purse steals trash; 'tis something, nothing;
> 'Twas mine, 'tis his, and has been slave to thousands;
> But he that filches from me my good name
> Robs me of that which not enriches him,
> And makes me poor indeed.

Peter H. Lewis, writing in the *New York Times* (December 25, 1990), has updated Iago's remarks for the computer age: "Who steals my personal computer steals cache, but he who filches from me my hard disk robs me of that which not enriches him, and makes me poor indeed."

Reputation is often tied up with honor. In *Richard II* (Act I, scene i) Thomas Mowbray, the Duke of Norfolk, is accused of treason and responds with this exposition on how mere accusation hurts both reputation and personal honor:

> The purest treasure mortal times afford
> Is spotless reputation; that away,
> Men are but gilded loam or painted clay.
> A jewel in a ten-times-barr'd-up chest
> Is a bold spirit in a loyal breast.
> Mine honor is my life, both grow in one;
> Take honor from me, and my life is done.

This is the origin of the phrase "spotless reputation." It is also a warning that to attack someone's honor is an attack on his or her life—professionally speaking.

Staff Popinjays

The frequent conflict between line officers (those who literally stand in the line of battle) and staff officers (those who work for the powers that be "behind the lines") has been well documented in both history and organization theory. Certainly the most famous denunciation of a staff "popinjay" comes from Shakespeare's *Henry IV, Part I* (Act I, scene iii). Hotspur, who has just led his men in a victorious but exhausting battle, is approached by a noncombatant staff officer demanding Hotspur's newly captured prisoners. He refuses to turn them over and is called to account for this seemingly insubordinate act. In his defense Hotspur tells King Henry IV of his contempt for such staff officers:

> My liege, I did deny no prisoners,
> But I remember, when the fight was done,
> When I was dry with rage and extreme toil,
> Breathless and faint, leaning upon my sword,
> Came there a certain lord, neat, and trimly dress'd,
> Fresh as a bridegroom, and his chin new reap'd
> Show'd like a stubble-land at harvest-home.
> He was perfumed like a milliner,
> And 'twixt his finger and his thumb he held
> A pouncet [perfume]-box, which ever and anon
> He gave his nose and took't away again,...
> And as the soldiers bore dead bodies by,
> He call'd them untaught knaves, unmannerly,
> To bring a slovenly unhandsome corse [corpse]

Betwixt the wind and his nobility.
With many holiday and lady terms
He questioned me, amongst the rest demanded
My prisoners in your Majesty's behalf.
I then, all smarting with my wounds being cold,
To be so pest'red with a popinjay,
Out of my grief [pain] and my impatience
Answer'd neglectingly, I know not what—
He should, or he should not—for he made me mad
To see him shine so brisk and smell so sweet,
And talk so like a waiting-gentlewoman
Of guns, and drums, and wounds.
              ...and but for these vile guns,
He would himself have been a soldier.

General James M. Gavin (who later served as chairman of the board of the Arthur D. Little, Inc., consulting firm) writes in his World War II memoir, *On to Berlin* (1978), that this was his "favorite description of a staff officer from a higher command." This was the one quotation from Shakespeare that you could traditionally expect a career army officer to know—if he was truly a gentleman as well as an officer.

Systems Analysis

Although he never used the term, Shakespeare understood the basics of systems analysis—the methodologically vigorous collection, manipulation and evaluation of organizational data. He knew that any analysis had to start with the present situation. As Lady Macbeth says in *Macbeth* (Act III, scene ii): "Things without all remedy should be without regard: what's done, is done."

Shakespeare knew that the analysis of any problem had to be approached without bias. Thus Hamlet says in *Hamlet* (Act II, scene ii): "There is nothing either good or bad, but thinking makes it so."

Shakespeare would also have been quite comfortable with the scientific method of today. After all, he has Fluellen exclaim in *Henry V* (Act V, scene i): "There is occasions and causes why and wherefore in all things."

The main reason to examine systems, whether organizational or mechanical, is to solve actual problems. In *The Merchant of Venice* (Act I, scene i) Bassanio offers this basic trouble-shooting technique:

> In my school-days, when I had lost one shaft [arrow],
> I shot his fellow of the self-same flight
> The self-same way with more advised watch
> To find the other forth, and by adventuring both,
> I oft found both.

Sometimes a "more advised watch" is all it takes—even today.

Though computers had not yet been invented, of course, Shakespeare could still be counted as a number cruncher. Statistics that portend the future, known as leading indicators, are among the most important analytical tools for economic and business projections. Though he is not usually credited with great mathematical acumen, it's fair to conclude that Shakespeare understood the basics for econometric projections. This is shown when he has Nestor state in *Troilus and Cressida* (Act I, scene iii):

> in such indexes (although small pricks
> To their subsequent volumes) there is seen
> The baby figure of the giant mass
> Of things to come at large.

Sometimes a systems analysis must be done instantaneously under dire circumstances. Perhaps the best example of this in any of Shakespeare's plays occurs toward the end of *Richard III*. King Richard, knowing that he is about to be defeated on the battlefield (Act V, scene iv), makes his famous shout for transportation: "A horse, a horse! my kingdom for a horse!" Why was he offering his kingdom for a mere horse? Because he had quickly analyzed the situation and realized his best course of action was to flee on horseback. His analysis was accurate. The fact that he was killed before he could act on his new data set does not take away from its essential correctness.

Timing Is Everything

Timing is crucial to business decisions. What will succeed in one time and context will fail in another, and vice versa. Sometimes it is all right to finish work ahead of time. As Ford says in *The Merry Wives of Windsor* (Act II, scene ii): "Better three hours too soon than a minute too late." But that may be inappropriate in many situations, particularly with inventory deliveries for "just-in-time" manufacturing systems. Then it is true, as Friar Lawrence advises Romeo in *Romeo and Juliet* (Act II, scene vi), that "too swift arrives as tardy as too slow."

Shakespeare knew that those who correctly timed their stratagems would win love, battle or fortune. For example, in *Othello* (Act II, scene iii) the villain, Iago, discourses on the critical nature of timing:

> How poor are they that have not patience!
> What wound did ever heal but by degrees?
> Thou know'st we work by wit, and not by witchcraft,
> And wit depends on dilatory time.

The inevitability of time was a constant theme in Shakespeare's work. In *Macbeth* (Act I, scene ii) the title character says as an aside:

> Come what come may,
> Time and the hour runs through the roughest day.

In Sonnet 60 Shakespeare observes:

128

Like as the waves make towards the pibbled [pebbled]
    shore,
So do our minutes hasten to their end.

But Shakespeare's definitive statement on time is made
by the fool Jaques meets in the forest in *As You Like It* (Act II,
scene vii):

"Good morrow, fool," quoth I. "No, sir," quoth he,
"Call me not fool till heaven hath sent me fortune."
And then he drew a dial [sundial] from his poke [pouch],
And looking on it, with lack-lustre eye,
Says very wisely, "It is ten a' clock;
Thus we may see," quoth he, "how the world wags.
'Tis but an hour ago since it was nine,
And after one hour more 'twill be eleven,
And so from hour to hour, we ripe and ripe,
And then from hour to hour, we rot and rot;
And thereby hangs a tale." When I did hear
The motley fool thus moral on the time,
My lungs began to crow like chanticleer [a rooster];
That fools should be so deep-contemplative,
And I did laugh sans intermission
An hour by his dial.

As far as timing is concerned, the fool agrees with Edgar
in *King Lear* (Act V, scene ii): "Ripeness is all." The Prince of
Denmark would have agreed. In *Hamlet* (Act V, scene ii) he
asserts that "the readiness is all." The problem with timing in

business life is that things don't always occur when we would desire them. Just think how often you have been given an ill-timed problem to solve and complained, like Prince Hamlet (Act I, scene v):

> The time is out of joint—O cursed spite,
> That ever I was born to set it right!

Tips and Bribes

Bribery is a common practice in business. When it is legal, it is merely called tipping—done "To Insure Promptness"—and does no harm. But some "tipping" is illegal and requires someone—such as a building inspector or police officer—to break a public trust. Today illegal drugs encourage astounding amounts of bribery. Shakespeare has Romeo in *Romeo and Juliet* (Act V, scene i) seek to buy an illegal drug, a poison, from a drugstore. The poor apothecary allows his "poverty" but not his "will" to consent to the deal.

ROMEO: Famine is in thy cheeks,
      Need and oppression starveth in thy eyes,
      Contempt and beggary hangs upon thy back;

```
                    The world is not thy friend, nor the world's
                        law,
                    The world affords no law to make thee rich;
                    Then be not poor, but break it, and take this.
    APOTHECARY:     My poverty, but not my will, consents.
```

Ironically, Romeo tells him that the gold he exchanges for the drug is

```
                    worse poison to men's souls,
        Doing more murther in this loathsome world,
        Than these poor compounds that thou mayest not sell.
```

Sales agents in virtually every industry engage in routine bribery, giving personal gifts to buyers. While only sometimes in cash, such "gifts" often have significant cash values. It is just as Shakespeare wrote in *The Merry Wives of Windsor* (Act II, scene ii): "If money go before, all ways do lie open." Shakespeare expanded upon this tactic in *The Winter's Tale* (Act IV, scene iv); Clown explains how to bribe someone of importance:

```
    He seems to be of great authority. Close with him,
    give him gold; and though authority be a stubborn
    bear; yet he is oft led by the nose with gold. Show
    the inside of your purse to the outside of his hand.
```

Fortunately, there are always some individuals who cannot be bought. Shakespeare was also familiar with those whose personal integrity and organizational loyalty were unimpeachable. Brutus in *Julius Caesar* was such a man. He explains that he would "rather be a dog" than take bribes (Act IV, scene iii):

> shall we now
> Contaminate our fingers with base bribes?
> And sell the mighty space of our large honors
> For so much trash as may be grasped thus?
> I had rather be a dog, and bay the moon,
> Than such a Roman.

Yet a Brutus is a rarity. He even complained (Act IV, scene iii) that his friend and co-conspirator Cassius was "much condemn'd to have an itching palm," then as now a "medical" condition that could only be temporarily cured by the pressing of coins into the hands. Nevertheless, most people are neither wholly honest nor wholly dishonest but somewhere in between. And that is not necessarily a bad thing. As Mariana says in *Measure for Measure* (Act V, scene i):

> They say best men are molded out of faults,
> And for the most, become much more the better
> For being a little bad.

Transformational Leadership

A transformational leader is one with the ability to change an imbedded organizational culture by creating a new vision for the organization and marshaling the appropriate support to make that vision the new reality. The best-known transformational leader is General George S. Patton, Jr., who during World War II took charge of a defeated and demoralized American army corps in North Africa and transformed it into a winning team. The task was different but no less difficult for Lee Iacocca, who took charge of a Chrysler Corporation on the verge of bankruptcy and disintegration and brought it back into profit. Similar challenges faced the leadership of AT&T when it went from a monopoly public utility to a company that had to change its corporate culture to compete in the open market.

In *Henry V* (Act V, scene ii) King Henry, in courting his future wife, Katherine, explains how they will be transformational leaders. When Katherine, the daughter of the king of France, explains in response to King Henry's demand for a kiss to seal their engagement that "it is not the fashion for the maids in France to kiss before they are married," King Henry assures her:

> O Kate, nice customs cur[t]sy to great kings. Dear
> Kate, you and I cannot be confin'd within the weak
> list [boundary] of a country's fashion. We are the
> makers of manners, Kate; and the liberty that
> follows our places stops the mouth of all find-faults.

The two things that all transformational leaders have in common are that they, as Shakespeare said, "are the makers of manners" and, because of "the liberty that follows" from the positions they hold, they have the power to "stop the mouth[s]" of those who would find fault with their reforms. Thus Shakespeare uses a request for a kiss as the basis for an analysis of why those who don't support organizational reforms can kiss off.

Since we're talking about Henry V and Katherine, note that she was the original "trophy wife"—not the modern kind (the young second wife of a much older, status-conscious executive) but the literal kind; Henry conquered France and brought her back as a "trophy."

Unity of Command

Only in the twentieth century has the long-known concept of unity of command, that the entire organization should be responsible to only one person, become firmly established as one of the most basic principles of management. But unity of command became conventional wisdom long ago. Shakespeare wrote of it in *King Lear* (Act II, scene iv); Regan (one of Lear's daughters) says:

> How in one house
> Should many people under two commands
> Hold amity? 'Tis hard, almost impossible.

Shakespeare knew that joint command, practiced in ancient Rome, all too often led to indecision and defeat. Niccolo Machiavelli, the greatest political analyst of the Italian Renaissance, wrote in 1517 that "it is better to confide any expedition to a single man of ordinary ability rather than to two even though they are men of the highest merit." Every military analyst since, from Napoleon Bonaparte to H. Norman Schwarzkopf, has agreed. When the modern corporation was created in the nineteenth century, it was structured on the military model of hierarchical command. While there are occasional deviations from this, they are the exception to the rule because, as Shakespeare wrote in *Coriolanus* (Act III, scene i):

> when two authorities are up,
> Neither supreme, how soon confusion
> May enter 'twixt the gap of both, and take
> The one by th' other.

Vaulting Ambition

Shakespeare's characters have contrasting attitudes about ambition. He often wrote about how it was the internally generated motivation needed for great accomplishment. In *Macbeth* (Act I, scene vii) he used an equine metaphor in a soliloquy by Macbeth that explains what starts him on murdering his way to the top:

> I have no spur
> To prick the sides of my intent, but only
> Vaulting ambition, which o'erleaps itself,
> And falls on th' other [side].

Ambition often ended in the death of the ambitious in Shakespeare's plays. For example, toward the end of *Henry IV, Part I* the Prince of Wales engages Hotspur in a deadly swordfight. As Hotspur dies (Act V, scene iv) the prince says:

> Ill-weav'd ambition, how much art thou shrunk!
> When that this body did contain a spirit,
> A kingdom for it was too small a bound,
> But now two paces of the vilest earth
> Is room enough.

The lesson here is that if you get too ambitious, your organizational rivals will gang up and declare war on you. Nowhere is this better illustrated than in *Julius Caesar*. Because the conspirators believe Caesar seeks to destroy the ancient Roman republic—because he is too ambitious—the conspirators slay him. Brutus justifies the assassination with these words to the citizens of Rome (Act III, scene ii):

As Caesar lov'd me, I weep for him; as he was fortunate, I rejoice at it; as he was valiant, I honor him: but, as he was ambitious, I slew him. There is tears for his love; joy for his fortune; honor for his valor; and death for his ambition.

Ambition in Shakespeare functions much like balance of power theory in international or organizational politics. As one party gets too strong and threatens to dominate the others, many of the smaller elements gang up to defeat the threat and restore the equilibrium. It is no different in office politics—only armies are smaller and the deaths fewer. After Brutus' denunciation of Caesar's ambition, Antony says in the same scene:

The noble Brutus
Hath told you Caesar was ambitious;
If it were so, it was a grievous fault,
And grievously hath Caesar answer'd it.

Of course the fault, as far as Caesar's friend Antony is concerned, was not so much that Caesar was ambitious, but that he frightened people by it—so much so that they were moved to murder. The lesson here: Don't flaunt ambition. Play it humble—at least until you are so strong that no one would dare move against you.

As is seen in both the tragedies of *Julius Caesar* and *Macbeth*, ambition often leads to the destruction of the ambitious; but a thwarted ambition sometimes led to repentance, as when Cardinal Wolsey in *Henry VIII* (Act III, scene ii) confesses his sins and advises:

> fling away ambition!
> By that sin fell the angels; how can man then
> (The image of his Maker) hope to win by it?
> Love thyself last, cherish those hearts that hate thee;
> Corruption wins not more than honesty.

But this is the deathbed confession of a loser, one who spent a career doing despicable things to advance his own and his king's ambition only to be eventually cast aside by that same king. The reality is that Shakespeare loved the ambitious, that he was extraordinarily ambitious himself, and that his plays mirror life then and now by showing the angst, folly, glory and downfall of ambitious characters the likes of which can still be found in any large organization.

Will to Succeed

Ever since Sigmund Freud introduced the subconscious mind to the modern world, countless self-help books have talked about the necessity of developing a winning attitude, of instilling within one's self or one's employees an internalized will to succeed. Their one common theme is that the power to do this lies within ourselves; to succeed we need only dig within to find it, psychologically speaking. Shakespeare, a Freudian even before Freud's time, has the villain Iago, in *Othello* (Act I, scene iii), assert that this "corrigible authority," this corrective power, "lies in our wills":

> 'Tis in ourselves that we are thus or thus. Our
> bodies are our gardens, to the which our wills are
> gardeners; so that if we will plant nettles or sow
> lettuce, set hyssop and weed up tine [wild grass],
> supply it with one gender of herbs or distract it
> with many, either to have it sterile with idleness or
> manur'd with industry—why, the power and
> corrigible authority of this lies in our wills.

"Manured with industry" is one of Shakespeare's least-quoted phrases—with good reason. To the modern ear *manure* means barnyard droppings. But Shakespeare's use of *manured* to mean *nurtured* implies that diligent effort will fertilize one's personal industry. The notion that hard work will allow us to control our fate is also examined in *Julius Caesar* (Act I, scene ii) when Cassius says:

The fault, dear Brutus, is not in our stars,
But in ourselves, that we are underlings.

This attitude of positive thinking may reflect Shakespeare's own. After all, he was a boy from the provinces who came to the big city (London) and rose to dominate one of its major industries (the theater) by the sheer force of hard work and will. Remember, he was known as *Will* Shakespeare.

Words of Honor and Dishonor

So much of business is based on the word of one person to another. In such "gentlemen's agreements" there is often no legal enforcement; thus the honor of one's word becomes all the more important. Perhaps the most gruesome statement of how willing one can be to keep one's word comes from Shakespeare's *Macbeth* (Act I, scene vii); Lady Macbeth tells her husband:

I have given suck, and know
How tender 'tis to love the babe that milks me;
I would, while it was smiling in my face,
Have pluck'd my nipple from his boneless gums,
And dash'd the brains out, had I so sworn as you
Have done to this.

This from a woman who would shortly die from what her husband diagnosed as "a mind diseased." But not every character in Shakespeare's plays has the perverted integrity of Lady Macbeth. Many are, as in modern business, just plain liars. For example, Queen Katherine in *Henry VIII* (Act IV, scene ii) remembers the promises of the deceased Cardinal Wolsey:

> His promises were, as he then was, mighty;
> But his performance, as he is now, nothing.

So often we are keenly aware that people are lying to us in business situations. After experience teaches us to catch such lies, we are frequently able to discern the truth. Shakespeare revealed one way to deal with the "world's false subtilties" in Sonnet 138:

> When my love swears that she is made of truth,
> I do believe her, though I know she lies,
> That she might think me some untutor'd youth,
> Unlearned in the world's false subtilties.

The world is such, according to Isabella's philosophy in *Measure for Measure* (Act II, scene iv), that:

> it oft falls out,
> To have what we would have,
> We speak not what we mean.

But by far the most scientific and studied liar in all of Shakespeare is Touchstone in *As You Like It*. When Jaques asks him to explain the various "degrees of the lie," he responds with this brief lecture on how to lie "by the book" (Act V, scene iv):

O sir, we quarrel in print, by the book—as you have books for good manners. I will name you the degrees. The first, the Retort Courteous; the second, the Quip Modest; the third, the Reply Churlish; the fourth, the Reproof Valiant; the fift[h], the Countercheck Quarrelsome; the sixt[h], the Lie with Circumstance; the seventh, the Lie Direct. All these you may avoid but the Lie Direct; and you may avoid that too, with an If. I knew when seven justices could not take [make] up a quarrel, but when the parties were met themselves, one of them thought but of an If, as, "If you said so, then I said so"; and they shook hands and swore brothers. Your If is the only peacemaker; much virtue in If.

Indeed there is. "What if?" questions are the underlying premise of many computer spreadsheet programs. However, the most famous "iffy" couplet was written not by Shakespeare, but by nineteenth-century American poet John Greenleaf Whittier:

For all sad words of tongue or pen,
The saddest are these: "It might have been!"

Working Stiffs

While Shakespeare's plays are justly famous for their stories of great men and great battles, most of his plays are peppered with vignettes of ordinary people. After all, he started out in life as just a working stiff himself, albeit in the theater. This must surely account for his sympathetic attitudes toward work and workers. In *King Lear* (Act V, scene iii) the essential nobility of all work is described by a captain:

> I cannot draw cart, nor eat dried oats,
> If it be man's work, I'll do it.

In *As You Like It* Shakespeare expands upon what is worthwhile "man's work." When Touchstone berates Corin, a shepherd, for not having been at court, Corin responds with his philosophy of working life (Act III, scene ii):

TOUCHSTONE: Wast ever in court, shepherd?

CORIN: No, truly....

TOUCHSTONE: Why, if thou never wast at court, thou never saw'st good manners; if thou never saw'st good manners, then thy manners must be wicked, and wickedness is sin, and sin is damnation. Thou art in a parlous state, shepherd.

CORIN: Not a whit, Touchstone. Those that are good manners at the court are as ridiculous in the country as the behavior of the country is most mockable at the court....

TOUCHSTONE: Thou art raw [crude].
CORIN: Sir, I am a true laborer: I earn that I eat, get that
    I wear, owe no man hate, envy no man's happiness,
    glad of other men's good, content with my harm
    [misfortunes], and the greatest of my pride is to see
    my ewes graze and my lambs suck.

Not all of us would be content being "a true laborer," as is Corin. It is therefore best that we take the attitude Autolycus takes in *The Winter's Tale* (Act IV, scene iv) when he observes similar men:

> How blessed are we that are not simple men!
> Yet nature might have made me as these are,
> Therefore I will not disdain.

Conflict between labor and management has frequently occurred when management has forgotten that laborers are people too. Emilia in *Othello* (Act IV, scene iii) makes this case in the context of marital relations. But if you allow that "husbands" equal management and "wives" equal workers, as they certainly did in the context of the times, then this is an apt description of labor-management conflict.

> But I do think it is their husbands' faults
> If wives do fall. Say that they slack their duties,
> And pour our treasures into foreign laps,
> Or else break out in peevish [silly] jealousies,
> Throwing restraint upon us; or say they strike us,

Or scant [reduce] our former having [allowances] in
  despite:
Why, we have galls [resentments]; and though we have
  some grace,
Yet have we some revenge. Let husbands know
Their wives have sense like them; they see, and smell,
And have their palates both for sweet and sour,
As husbands have.

Finally, Shakespeare often allows his workmen to banter
with the nobility to show that they can be every bit as bright
and witty as their "betters." This minor effort at subverting
the social order is no better illustrated than in this scene from
Julius Caesar (Act I, scene i), when Flavius and Marullus, Roman officials, take to task "mechanicals" (workers) for being
improperly dressed.

FLAVIUS: What, know you not,
                  Being mechanical, you ought not walk
                  Upon a laboring day without the sign
                  Of your profession? Speak, what trade art
                    thou?
CARPENTER: Why, sir, a carpenter.
MARULLUS: Where is thy leather apron and thy rule?
                  What dost thou with thy best apparel on?
                  You, sir, what trade are you?
COBBLER: Truly, sir, in respect of a fine workman, I am
                  but, as you would say, a cobbler [bungler].
MARULLUS: But what trade art thou? Answer me directly.

COBBLER:	A trade sir, that I hope I may use with a safe conscience; which is indeed, sir, a mender of bad soles.
MARULLUS:	What trade, thou knave? thou naughty knave, what trade?...
FLAVIUS:	Thou art a cobbler [shoemaker], art thou?
COBBLER:	Truly, sir, all that I live by is with the awl: I meddle with no tradesman's matters, nor women's matters; but withal I am indeed, sir, a surgeon to old shoes....
FLAVIUS:	But wherefore art not in thy shop to-day? Why dost thou lead these men about the streets?
COBBLER:	Truly, sir, to wear out their shoes, to get myself into more work.

Surely this was one cobbler (shoemaker) who wasn't a cobbler (bungler). He knew how to encourage new business. No doubt he gave it his awl. As this book has—for this is all of *Shakespeare on Management*.

General Index

Adam, *As You Like It*, 103, 108–9
Agincourt, Battle of, 20, 45
Aguecheek, Sir Andrew, *Twelfth Night*, 56
Albany, Duke of, *Lear*, 76
All's Well That Ends Well, 3, 101
Ambition, 136–38
Angelo, *Measure for Measure*, 34
Angus, *Macbeth*, 30
Antonio, *Merchant of Venice*, 73, 90, 91
Antony, Mark, *Julius Caesar*, 11–13, 55, 76, 82, 99–100, 137
Antony, Mark, *Antony and Cleopatra*, 48–49, 56, 116
Antony and Cleopatra, 48, 56, 82, 116
As You Like It, 18, 39, 67, 103, 108, 113, 118, 129, 142, 143
Autolycus, *Winter's Tale*, 94, 144

Balance of power, 137
Banquo, *Macbeth*, 81
Baptista, *Taming of the Shrew*, 5
Bardolph, *Henry IV, Part II*, 68
Bassanio, *Merchant of Venice*, 1, 34, 87, 91, 126
Belch, Sir Toby, *Twelfth Night*, 56
Benefit-cost analysis, 87
Berowne, *Love's Labor's Lost*, 66
Blass, Bill, 23
Body language, 107

Bolingbroke, Henry, *Richard II*, 56
Borachio, *Much Ado*, 6–7
Bosworth Field, Battle of, 84
Bottom, *Midsummer Night's Dream*, 2
Brand extension, 23
Bribery, 34, 130–32
Brutus, *Julius Caesar*, 21, 35–36, 43, 76, 85–86, 132, 137
Brutus, *Coriolanus*, 76
Buckingham, Duke of, *Richard III*, 107
Bureaucracy, 27–28

Cade, Jack, *Henry VI, Part II*, 107
Canterbury, Archbishop of, *Henry V*, 28
Cassio, *Othello*, 2, 122
Cassius, *Julius Caesar*, 13, 43, 85–86, 132, 139–40
Celia, *As You Like It*, 18
Chief Justice, *Henry IV, Part II*, 40
Cicero, *Julius Caesar*, 85–86
Claudio, *Much Ado*, 67, 72
Claudius, *Hamlet*, 25, 33–34, 63, 88
Cleopatra, *Antony and Cleopatra*, 48, 49
Confrontation meetings, 55–56
Conrade, *Much Ado*, 6–7
Constance, *King John*, 103
Contingency planning, 84–85
Cordelia, *Lear*, 99

Corin, *As You Like it*, 143–44
Coriolanus, *Coriolanus*, 34
Coriolanus, 4, 76, 120, 135
Costard, *Love's Labor's Lost*, 105
Cressida, *Troilus and Cressida*, 73, 107
Cymbeline, 22, 32, 81

Decius, *Julius Caesar*, 16
Dick the butcher, *Henry VI, Part II*, 32–33
Discrimination, 7–10, 26
Dispute settlement, 119–21
Disraeli, Benjamin, 18
Diversification, 90
Duke Vincentio, *Measure for Measure*, 30–31
Duncan, *Macbeth*, 24, 42

Econometric projections, 127
Edgar, *Lear*, 50, 129
Edmund, *Lear*, 8, 10, 43, 79
Efficiency report, 75–78
Elizabeth I, 34, 50
Emilia, *Othello*, 72, 144
Executive angst, 38

Falstaff, Sir John, *Henry IV, Parts I and II*, 14–15, 40, 79–80, 96–98, 114, 122
Fenton, *Merry Wives*, 53, 55
Fiduciary relationships, 79
Flavius, *Julius Caesar*, 145–46
Fluellen, *Henry V*, 126
Ford, Francis, *Merry Wives*, 128
Francis, Friar, *Much Ado*, 82
Free speech, 35

Gaunt, John of, *Richard II*, 74
Gertrude, *Hamlet*, 98, 111

Gloucester, Richard, Duke of, *Henry VI, Part III*, 95–96
Gloucester, Earl of, *Lear*, 8
Goneril, *Lear*, 51, 76
Good will, 121
Gossip, 70
Government regulation, 58
Gratiano, *Merchant of Venice*, 87

Hamlet, *Hamlet*, 23, 25, 27, 31, 36, 41–42, 88–89, 97–98, 100, 104, 107, 111, 126, 129–30
Hamlet, 3, 23, 25, 27, 31, 33–36, 41, 63, 67, 78, 88–89, 95, 98, 100, 101, 104, 107, 111, 114, 120, 126, 129
Harrington, John, 35
Hawthorne experiments, 30
Helicanus, *Pericles*, 16
Henry IV, *Henry IV, Parts I and II*, 34, 38, 51–52, 56, 60–61, 76, 124
Henry IV, Part I, 14, 67, 69–70, 76, 79–80, 83, 96, 122, 124, 136
Henry IV, Part II, 38, 40, 42, 47, 51–52, 60, 63, 68, 77–78, 82, 87, 114, 118, 120
Henry V, *Henry IV, Parts I and II; Henry V*, 20, 36–37, 39, 45, 51–52, 60–62, 76–78, 83–84, 122, 133, 134, 136
Henry V, 20, 28, 36, 39, 45, 51, 61, 126, 133
Henry VI, Part II, 32
Henry VI, Part III, 52, 95
Henry VIII, 81, 102, 109, 138
Hermione, *Winter's Tale*, 104
Hero, *Much Ado*, 72
Holofernes, *Love's Labor's Lost*, 98
Horatio, *Hamlet*, 31

Hortensio, *Taming of the Shrew*, 81, 116

Hotspur (Henry Percy), *Henry IV, Part I*, 66, 124, 136

Iacocca, Lee, 100, 133

Iago, *Othello*, 17, 22, 72, 82, 94, 102, 122–23, 128, 139

Imogen, *Cymbeline*, 81

In Search of Excellence, 44

Indecisiveness, 25, 41–43

Industrial democracy, 39

Isabella, *Measure for Measure*, 42, 59, 101, 141

Jaques, *As You Like It*, 113, 129, 142

Job design, 82

Juliet, *Romeo and Juliet*, 91, 105

Julius Caesar, *Julius Caesar*, 11, 13–14, 16–17, 83, 136–137

Julius Caesar, 11, 12–14, 16, 21, 35–36, 43, 69, 76, 83, 84, 99, 132, 136–37, 138, 139, 145

Katherine, *Taming of the Shrew*, 5, 27, 53, 55

Katherine, *Henry V*, 20, 133, 134

Katherine, *Henry VIII*, 141

King John, 74, 103

King Lear, 8, 41, 43, 50–51, 60, 70, 75, 76, 79, 99, 109–10, 116, 129, 134, 143

Kiss Me Kate, 53

Laertes, *Hamlet*, 36, 78, 95

Lawrence, Friar, *Romeo and Juliet*, 22, 128

Leading indicators, 127

Lear, King, *Lear*, 50–51, 70, 99, 109–10

Leveraged buyouts, 58

Lewis, Peter H., 123

Livingston, J. Sterling, 73

Lorenzo, *Merchant of Venice*, 64

Love's Labor's Lost, 66, 98, 105

Lucentio, *Taming of the Shrew*, 65

Lucio, *Measure for Measure*, 5, 43, 88

Macbeth, *Macbeth*, 24, 30, 34, 42, 70, 81, 88, 111, 115, 128, 136

Macbeth, Lady, *Macbeth*, 26, 34, 42, 100, 126, 140–41

Macbeth, 24–25, 26, 30, 41, 42, 50, 57, 58, 69–70, 81, 88, 106, 111, 115, 126, 128, 136, 138, 140

Machiavelli, Niccolo, 25, 96, 135

Malvolio, *Twelfth Night*, 6, 103

Management consultants, 81

Management training, 116

Mariana, *Measure for Measure*, 132

Marullus, *Julius Caesar*, 145–46

Measure for Measure, 5, 30–31, 34, 42, 43, 59, 64, 88, 101, 132, 141

Menenius, *Coriolanus*, 76, 120

Merchant of Venice, The, 1, 8, 10, 21, 23–24, 34, 64, 73, 80, 87, 90, 91–93, 126

Merit promotion, 101

Merry Wives of Windsor, The, 53, 55, 128, 131

Midsummer Night's Dream, A, 2

Miles, Rufus E., Jr., 74

Morocco, Prince of, *Merchant of Venice*, 8, 21

Mowbray, Thomas, Duke of Norfolk, *Richard II*, 19, 123

Much Ado About Nothing, 6, 67, 72, 82

Nestor, *Troilus and Cressida*, 127
Norfolk, Duke of, *Henry VIII*, 101
Northumberland, Earl of, *Henry VI, Part III*, 42, 47
Number cruncher, 127

Octavius Caesar, *Julius Caesar*, 16
On to Berlin, 125
Ophelia, *Hamlet*, 36, 114
Organization theory, 29
Organizational politics, 137
Orlando, *As You Like It*, 103, 108
Othello, *Othello*, 72, 94, 108, 122
Othello, 2, 17, 22, 72, 82, 94, 102, 108, 122, 128, 139, 144

Page, Anne, *Merry Wives*, 53, 55
Paris, *Troilus and Cressida*, 66
Parolles, *All's Well*, 101
Participative management, 60
Passionate Pilgrim, 17
Path-goal leadership, 62
Pericles, 16, 58
Peters, Tom, 44
Petruchio, *Taming of the Shrew*, 5, 10, 27, 53, 55
Philip the Bastard, *King John*, 74
Pisanio, *Cymbeline*, 22
Polonius, *Hamlet*, 3, 78, 95, 98, 104
Portia, *Merchant of Venice*, 80, 91–93
Positive thinking, 140
Posthumus, *Cymbeline*, 32
Prenuptial agreement, 11
Probate, 10
Productivity, 64
Psychological stroking, 104

Rape of Lucrece, 114
Regan, *Lear*, 116, 134
Rewards, 101, 105
Richard II, *Richard II*, 11, 64, 111–12, 120
Richard II, 11, 19, 50, 56, 64, 74, 111, 120, 123
Richard III, *Richard III*, 34, 56, 84, 95–96, 127. *See also* Gloucester, Richard
Richard III, 34, 50, 58, 84, 95, 107, 108, 127
Romeo, *Romeo and Juliet*, 22, 128, 130–31
Romeo and Juliet, 22, 91, 105, 128, 130–31
Rosalind, *As You Like It*, 67

Sales techniques, 66–67
Scientific management, 74
Seniority, 102
Sex discrimination, 26
Shallow, *Henry IV, Part II*, 82
Shylock, *Merchant of Venice*, 4, 8, 23–24, 73, 80, 91–92
Smith, Adam, 29
Social drinking, 2
Social security, 108–9
Stephano, *Tempest*, 80
Sunk costs, 88

Taming of the Shrew, The, 5, 10, 27, 53, 55, 65, 81, 82, 112, 116
Taylor, Frederick, 74
Tempest, The, 80
Third-party arbitration, 119
Thriving on Chaos, 44
Timon, *Timon of Athens*, 80, 94
Timon of Athens, 80, 87, 94

Too Funny to Be President, 9
Touchstone, *As You Like It*, 142, 143–44
Tranio, *Taming of the Shrew*, 82, 112
Troilus and Cressida, 28, 66, 73, 107, 127
Trophy wife, 134
Trouble-shooting, 126
True laborer, 144
Truth in advertising, 7
Tucker, Sophie, 38
Twelfth Night, 6, 56, 103

Udall, Morris K., 9
Ulysses, *Troilus and Cressida*, 28, 66, 107

Wales, Prince of, *see* Henry V
Warwick, Earl of, *Henry IV, Part II*, 118
Wealth of Nations, The, 29
Western Electric Company, 30
Whittier, John Greenleaf, 142
Wills, 10–13
Winter's Tale, A, 94, 104, 131, 144
Wolsey, Cardinal, *Henry VIII*, 109, 138, 141
Workaholic, 13
Worst-case scenario, 85

York, Archbishop of, *Richard III*, 128

Quotation Index

A friend i' the court is better than a penny in purse, 82

A horse! a horse! my kingdom for a horse, 127

A pound of that same merchant's flesh is thine, 92

All the world's a stage, 113

apparel oft proclaims the man, 3

as adversaries do in law, 112

As Caesar loved me, 137

As you are old and reverend, you should be wise, 51

Assume a virtue, if you have it not, 111

baby figure of the giant mass, 127

Be not afraid of greatness, 103

best men are moulded out of faults, 132

Betwixt the wind and his nobility, 125

better part of valor is discretion, 97

blasted with antiquity, 40

Bloody instructions, 24

borrowing dulleth th' edge of husbandry, 78

busy giddy minds, 60

but for these vile guns, 125

Caesar was ambitious, 137

conscience does make cowards of us all, 89

constant service of the antique world, 103

consumption of the purse, 80

Contaminate our fingers with base bribes, 132

Costly thy habit as thy purse can buy, 3

Cowards die many times before their deaths, 83

crushing penury, 112

Cry, "God for Harry, England, and Saint George!" 62

curse of service, 102

death for his ambition, 137

Dishonor not your mothers, 61

each thing's a thief, 94–95

Eat no onions nor garlic, 2

elder I wax, the better I shall appear, 39

Even in the cannon's mouth, 113

Every good servant does not all commands, 32

excellent foppery [foolishness] of the world, 43

False face must hide, 111

Famine is in thy cheeks, 130
fashion wears out more apparel than the man, 7
fault, dear Brutus, is not in our stars, 43, 140
fewer men, the greater share of honor, 45
flattery is the bellows blows up sin, 16
Fortune brings in some boats that are not steer'd, 22
Friends, Romans, countrymen, 11
Friendship is constant in all other things, 73
Frosty but kindly, 39
full of sound and fury, 115

game's afoot, 62
glass of fashion, 114
God has given you one face, 107
green-eyed monster, 72

Had I but serv'd my God, 109
Hath not a Jew eyes? 8
he that filches from me my good name, 122
He thinks too much: such men are dangerous, 13
Here was a Caesar! When comes such another? 12
His promises were, as he then was, mighty, 141
his will is not his own, 36
Hold thy desperate hand, 22
honest in nothing but in his clothes, 5
Honor is a mere scutcheon, 97
How sour sweet music is, 64

I am in blood, 88
I am not naturally honest, 94
I can counterfeit the deep tragedian, 107
I come to wive it wealthily in Padua, 53
I had rather be a dog, and bay the moon, 132
I have given suck, 140
I have turn'd away my former self, 78
I only speak right on, 99
If all the year were playing holidays, 84
If it be man's work, I'll do it, 143
If sack and sugar be a fault, God help the wicked! 15
If we are mark'd to die, we are enow, 45
If you can look into the seeds of time, 81
If you prick us, do we not bleed? 24
I'll cavil on the ninth part of a hair, 66
in such indexes, although small pricks, 127
it was a grievous fault, 137

laid on with a trowel, 18
Lechery, sir, it provokes, and unprovokes, 130
left me naked to mine enemies, 109
Let no such man be trusted, 65
Let us, like merchants, first show foul wares, 65
let's kill all the lawyers, 32–33
Let's reason with the worst that may befall, 85

Life's but a walking shadow, 115
Like as the waves make towards the
    pibbled shore, 129
little touch of Harry in the night, 45
loan oft loses both itself and friend,
    78
lowliness is young ambition's ladder,
    36

make guilty of our disasters the sun,
    the moon and the stars, 43
many fresh streams meet in one salt
    sea, 29
marriage of true minds, 55
Mend your speech a little, 99
mender of bad soles, 146
mince not the general tongue, 49
Mine honor is my life, 123
Mislike me not for my complexion,
    8
More honor'd in the breach than
    the observance, 31
More matter, with less art, 98
music for the time doth change his
    nature, 64
music oft hath such a charm, 64
my ewes graze and my lambs suck,
    144
My poverty, but not my will,
    consents, 131

nature of bad news infects the
    teller, 49
Neither a borrower nor a lender be,
    78
nice customs curtsy to great kings,
    133
No profit grows where is no
    pleasure ta'en, 82

noblest Roman of them all, 76
Now, gods, stand up for bastards! 9

Once more unto the breach, 61
One good deed dying tongueless,
    104
one man in his time plays many
    parts, 113
only old in judgement and
    understanding, 40
Our bodies are our gardens, 139
Our doubts are traitors, 43, 88
Our praises are our wages, 104

play I in one person many people,
    112
play's the thing, 101
policy sits above conscience, 87
Presume not that I am the thing I
    was, 77

quality of mercy is not strained, 80

readiness is all, 129
Reputation is an idle and most false
    imposition, 122
Returning were as tedious as go
    o'er, 88
Ripeness is all, 129
Rude am I in my speech, 108

Save ceremony, save general
    ceremony? 37
screw you courage to the sticking
    place, 42
sea of troubles, 41
Seeking the bubble reputation, 113
Sell when you can: you are not for
    all markets, 67

set the murtherous Machevil to school, 96
sharper than a serpent's tooth, 110
Show the inside of your purse, 131
Signifying nothing, 115
Sleek-headed men and such as sleep a-nights, 13
slings and arrows of outrageous fortune, 41
smell as sweet, 105
some have greatness thrust upon them, 103
Speak the speech, I pray you, 100
speechless death, 19
spotless reputation, 123
strict statutes and most biting laws, 31
struts and frets his hour upon the stage, 115
Suit the action to the word, 100
surgeon to old shoes, 146
Sweet are the uses of adversity, 118

take my milk for gall, 26
Talkers are no good doers, 108
thankless child, 110
that strumpet fortune, 103
that which we call a rose, 105
There is a tide in the affairs of men, 21
There is nothing either good or bad, 126
thereby hangs a tale, 129
thinks men honest that but seem to be so, 94
This day is call'd the feast of Crispian, 45
This story shall the good man teach his son, 46

Those he commands move only in command, 30
Thou call'dst me dog before thou hadst a cause, 74
Thou shalt have justice, more than thou desir'st, 92
Though I look old, yet I am strong and lusty, 39
Time and the hour runs through the roughest day, 128
time is out of joint, 130
To be, or not to be, 41
To beguile the time, 106
To business that we love we rise betime, 82
to the manner born, 31
to thine own self be true, 95
too swift arrives as tardy as too slow, 128
trippingly on the tongue, 100
trust no agent, 67
Two stars keep not their motion in one sphere, 70

Unburthen'd crawl toward death, 110
Uneasy lies the head that wears the crown, 38
unsex me here, 26
Upon the fortune of the present year, 90
upon this bank and shoal of time, 24
use them according to their desert, 104

villainy you teach me, I will execute, 24

We are the makers of manners, 133

155

We cannot all be masters, 17

We few, we happy few, we band of brothers, 46

we quarrel in print, by the book, 142

We speak not what we mean, 141

We were not born to sue, but to command, 120

what a deformed thief this fashion is, 6

what's done is done, 126

When forty winters shall besiege thy brow, 39

When shall we three meet again, 57

When sorrows come, they come not single spies, 63

When the hurly-burly's done, 57

who should 'scape whipping? 104

Who steals my purse steals trash, 122

why and wherefore in all things, 126

Will Fortune never come with both hands full, 63

wit depends on dilatory time, 128

Words are easy, like the wind, 17

world is not thy friend, 131

world's false subtilties, 141

Yet herein will I imitate the sun, 76

Yond Cassius has a lean and hungry look, 13